Be an Island

Be an Island

The Buddhist Practice of Inner Peace

Ayya Khema

Foreword by Sandy Boucher

Wisdom Publications • Boston

Wisdom Publications

199 Elm Street

Somerville, Massachusetts 02144 USA

Passages from the *Mahāparinibbāna Sutta* in the preface adapted from *The Last Days of the Buddha.* (Kandy: Buddhist Publication Society, 1988)

Verses from the *Dhammapada* on page 23 translated by Ven. Khantipalo.

Library of Congress Cataloging-in-Publication Data
Khema, Ayya.
      Be an island : the Buddhist practice of inner peace / by Ayya Khema.
          p.   cm.
      ISBN 0-86171-147-5 (pbk. : alk. paper)
          1. Spiritual life—Buddhism—Psychological aspects.
      2. Peace of mind—Religious aspects—Buddhism.   3. Buddhism—Doctrines.
      I. Title.
      BQ5612.K44 1999
      294.3'444—DC21   98-40893

ISBN 0-86171-147-5

04   03   02   01   00
6   5   4   3

Cover image: *View of the Shimmering Sea from Woods Hole, Massachusetts,* Feodor Zakharov, ca. 1927, Collection of Duke University Museum of Art

Designed by: Jennie Malcolm

Wisdom Publications' books are printed on acid-free paper and meet the guidelines for the permanence and durability of the Committee on Production Guidelines for Book Longevity of the Council on Library Resources.

Printed in the United States of America

Contents

Publisher's Acknowledgment

The publisher gratefully acknowledges the generous help of the Hershey Family Foundation in sponsoring the printing of this book. ॐ

Foreword

*I*n the great adventure of Buddhism's coming to the West, one of the most fascinating developments has been its meeting with feminism. The relationship that developed between the two, while sometimes thorny, has enriched both endeavors immeasurably. Sister Ayya Khema, one of the first generation of Western women teachers, contributed powerfully to this conjunction; an American citizen born in northern Europe, she will be remembered most vividly for her championing of the cause of Buddhist nuns.

Ayya Khema was a strong, independent woman who survived early hardship. As a German-Jewish child in the Second World War she knew prejudice, imprisonment, and the death of her father. As a married woman she worked a farm in Australia while raising her children. She then founded a Theravada Buddhist forest monastery there and took the robes, shaving her head and donning the brown cloth of a renunciant. Her new name, Khema, had belonged to a nun alive during the Buddha's lifetime who had been known for her great insight and verbal ability and had been cited by the Buddha as providing a standard for right conduct. Ayya Khema radiated confidence; her being a woman never impeded her study and practice of Dhamma. She penetrated deeply into the practice and communicated the fruits of her insights with great clarity in her public talks and private instruction. That her own Theravada tradition denied her full ordination, that nuns in Southeast Asian countries were neglected and ill-served by their tradition—these injustices turned Ayya Khema into an activist. She did not choose the battle, but, self-respecting as she was, she stood up for her own dignity and that of all women. As a sincere practitioner and a powerful spokesperson, she became one of the Western Buddhist teachers who has truly made a difference in this century.

To be involved in the publishing of this book takes me back to another book preparation twelve years ago on Parappuduwa Nuns Island in Ratgama Lake in Sri Lanka. In the damp, tropical heat, I sat on a verandah surrounded by extravagant jungle vegetation and pored over the proofs of a book of Ayya's Dhamma talks to be published by a group of Sri Lankan donors. That rustling in the underbrush, I knew, signaled the progress of a giant monitor lizard lumbering past; the wild screeches piercing the air came from brilliantly hued birds perched in the low trees.

Ayya Khema, stout in her brown robe, her head shaved clean, leaned over me to confer on some very strange wording that could only have been produced by a typesetter to whom the English language was an exotic challenge. Ayya would frown as she concentrated on the mangled phrase, and then, often, as we sorted it out, our consternation would dissolve into laughter.

My proofreading occupied only a few hours of each day. Up at 4 A.M., we *anagarikas* (eight-precept nuns) donned our white robes, lit our kerosene lanterns, and trudged in thick darkness to the top of the island's solitary hill, to enter the *bhāvanā sala* or meditation hall. At the front of the room we could barely discern the immobile form of Ayya Khema, deep in meditation. Gradually brightness gathered in the room; birds awoke, announcing their presence with cascades of sound; and Ayya became visible, her head raised, face suffused with joy, a lightness like a benediction.

Thus our day began, and progressed through sutta study with Ayya and a single, ceremonially served meal, sometimes brought to us by the villagers on the lake shore, sometimes prepared for us by our Sri Lankan cook. As the sun fell behind the tall trees bordering the lake, we again sat in meditation, and listened to Ayya expound upon an aspect of the Buddha's teachings. Then we ended our day with chanting, Ayya's voice strongly guiding us, first through the unfamiliar Pali syllables, then through the English translations. We chanted, for instance,

> *Even as a mother protects, with her life,*
> *Her child, her only child,*
> *So with a boundless heart*
> *Should one cherish all living beings:*
> *Radiating kindness over the entire world . . .*

One of Ayya's great contributions is her founding of Buddhist centers. As one student put it, "You know how when the baby Buddha walked, at each step a lotus sprang up? Well, everywhere Ayya Khema goes, a meditation center springs up." She began in 1978 with the forest monastery Wat Buddha Dhamma in New South Wales, Australia. Then in the eighties in Sri Lanka she formed the International Buddhist Women's Center and founded the nunnery Parappuduwa Nuns Island at the invitation of the Sri Lankan government. She did so in order to provide Western women with a Buddhist monastic experience in a Buddhist country: to offer us silence, safety, concentration, inner spaciousness. With her German students she created Buddha Haus. And as her death neared, she established Metta Vihara, a monastery to accommodate both men and women, the first Theravada monastery in Germany.

Ayya savored the peace and enclosure of monastic life, yet she was willing, in the middle of our rains retreat, to leave Parappuduwa Nuns Island and fly to the United States to speak on a panel on Women and Buddhism at a prestigious academic Buddhist-Christian convocation. When she returned to the island, at our request she shared the tape of her panel with us. On the tape Ayya spoke briefly and concisely about the situation of women in Buddhist traditions. She told the truth in blunt, no-nonsense terms, and I remember thinking how extremely radical and brave she was in doing so. But it was in the question-and-answer period that she captivated us and provoked a roar of approving laughter. A male questioner wondered, in a tone intended to trivialize and dismiss the whole subject of the panel, why there should be a *separate* panel comprised only of women, to address the issue of women and Buddhism. Why couldn't the topic be incorporated into the other discussions? One panelist began a tempered, careful response, and then Ayya's voice cut in, its tone balanced just on the edge of annoyance. Perhaps the questioner should ask instead, she suggested, why almost every one of the other panels at the conference was composed exclusively of *men* and excluded all concerns specific to women! That would be a more productive inquiry, she concluded. And the subject was closed. One could only imagine the look on the man's face as the room erupted in applause and amusement.

Ayya did not dislike individual men—indeed she had loyal male students—but she hated the hardship visited on women by the male supremacy endemic to Buddhism. Quick-witted, strongly grounded in what she knew, and unafraid, Ayya Khema could be formidable.

Her forthrightness could cause friction with students and associates. Women who came to the Nuns Island wanting a warm, motherly mentor found instead a strong exponent of the Dhamma, a demanding teacher, and a consistent spiritual companion. Ayya Khema did not hesitate to speak her mind and assumed that we novices could handle what came our way and stay focused on our practice. Some people found Ayya Khema's manner authoritarian and brusque, and at times people's feelings were hurt by her treatment of them. I believe Ayya Khema was not much interested in personality, her own or anyone else's: she focused always on the goals of liberation and equality, and she emphasized the necessity to cleave to practice. Sometimes this prevented her from attending to the complexity of human relationships and opening to others' limitations and perspectives. She was flawed, as we all are; at the same time she lived a life of immense value to others.

꙳ Ayya Khema taught often in the United States, particularly in California, where one of her daughters lived. I first met her at Dhamma Dena, the meditation center in the Mojave Desert headed by Ruth Denison. Years after my stay on the Nuns Island, I sat with Ayya Khema in Santa Fe, New Mexico, and at Green Gulch Farm in California. During this time she was establishing a center in Germany, and she regularly went to Europe to teach. Often she spoke at the conferences and events sponsored by Sakyadhita, the international association of Buddhist women, which she had helped to found. (I think Ayya would be amused to discover that she has already found her way onto the Internet. At a site called "Sakyadhita," next to an image of the celestial bodhisattva Kwan Yin, appears a color photograph of a smiling Ayya Khema, and below it some remarks of hers entitled "Revival of Bhikkhuni (nuns) Ordination in Sri Lanka.")

This human life is short, Ayya reminded us, and the priority is to get on with the practice. She embodied the Theravadin concept that the teachings matter, not the teacher. This insistence upon the message rather than the messenger informs Ayya Khema's many books, which have been published in English and German and translated into numerous other languages. They are all, with the exception of a recently published autobiography, collections of her Dhamma talks. Her genius as a teacher lay in her ability to present the essence of the Buddha's teachings in simple, accessible prose. This she did without notes or sources of any kind, quoting frequently from the suttas, speaking distinctly, in a strong voice, as her large eyes assessed her audience. She was an impressive, inspiring exponent of the timeless wisdom of the Buddha's teachings. Her printed talks, including the ones in this volume, reflect her conviction and clarity.

In 1988, at the Chinese Hsi Lai Temple near Los Angeles, Ayya Khema received full ordination in the nuns' lineage that extends back to the *theris*, the enlightened women ordained by the Buddha himself. Ordination within this Chinese lineage in most cases is not accepted by the Southeast Asian Theravada sanghas of monks—Ayya's tradition—but it was the only ordination open to her. One can argue that ordination is an external gesture that is meaningless in terms of actual spiritual attainment, but Ayya Khema understood its importance for the validation of her own and other women's efforts; women so utterly committed to the path of Buddhist renunciation deserved to be recognized by the worldly establishment of their tradition.

Over the years Ayya Khema spoke up for ordination of Theravada nuns on several continents and in countless gatherings great and small. She pointed out that without full ordination the nuns are, particularly in the eyes of Asian communities, spiritual nonentities, not deserving of material support, proper training in Dhamma, or the respect accorded the monks. As so visible a spokeswoman, Ayya drew much critical fire, yet she never sacrificed her convictions in order to be accepted by the Southeast Asian Buddhist establishment. She will be best remembered for this campaign she waged. Her name and her efforts are known throughout the Buddhist world, wherever there are women in robes. Indeed the changes in attitude and behavior toward nuns that have come about, still partial and gradual in many areas but happening nevertheless, are the result of the activism and strong inspiration of Ayya Khema and a few other valiant and determined female renunciants. Her example and her message have kindled a light in the hearts of countless women who had been inured to second-class status and official neglect, and showed them a way to express their full humanity. Nothing could be more essentially Buddhist than spiritual equality regardless of gender; Ayya Khema knew that in challenging the establishment she expressed the deeper truth of Buddhist teachings.

In the almost fifteen years I knew Ayya Khema my respect for her grew. Her fidelity to her chosen path never faltered, her mistakes were honest ones, her limitations no worse than mine and her strengths far exceeding any I could imagine possessing. Remembering her now, as I last saw her, dying of cancer yet fully alive and focused on her task, I realize my respect for her had deepened to love. She was a woman of great heart and vision, and unshakable courage. She was one of Buddha's lions. May her roar echo in these pages and out across the world to generations of followers-of-the-way to come.

Sandy Boucher ॐ November 1998

Preface

$\mathcal{B}$efore the Buddha died, 2,500 years ago, he gave a last discourse. This talk is recounted in the *Mahā Parinibbāna Sutta (Great Passing Discourse)* and is preserved in the Pali canon, the sacred books of Buddhism. During his ministry of forty-five years the Buddha had taught all that was necessary to reach the goal of liberation. In this last phase of his life his primary concern was to impress on his disciples the need to put those same teachings into practice.

In the *Mahā Parinibbāna Sutta,* when Ānanda, his cousin and faithful attendant, voices his hope that the Buddha will give some last instructions to the community of monks and nuns, the Buddha tells him that he has withheld nothing "with the closed fist of a teacher who keeps some things back." And he emphasizes that his disciples need not depend on him for leadership: "Therefore, Ananda, be islands unto yourselves, refuges unto yourselves, seeking no external refuge; with the Dhamma as your island, the Dhamma as your refuge."

He then goes on, "Those disciples of mine, Ānanda, who now or after I am gone, abide as an island unto themselves…having the Dhamma as their island and refuge…it is they who will become the highest [enlightened], if they have the desire to learn."

The twenty-four talks in this book are given in the spirit of the *Mahā Parinibbāna Sutta* and are all aimed at our own practice, "having the Dhamma as our island and refuge." While they elaborate and interpret the Buddha's words, they are based on his discourses and his answers to questions.

The first chapter helps us understand what it means to "take refuge" in the Buddha, Dhamma, and Sangha. The second chapter begins with an expression of homage and trust in the Dhamma and goes on to describe the inner opening of heart and mind we need to "seek no other refuge." Both chapters appear at the beginning of the book as an offering, which we may use or not, as we see fit. Having finished the book, we may return to them and find them more meaningful.

Perhaps we will find only a few of the other chapters helpful at the present moment. But that too will be a great opening, nonetheless, because the Dhamma will have then become a part of our inner life and can grow and expand until it becomes all of us.

᠃ My thanks go to all the nuns, anagarikas, and the lay men and women who have listened time and again to my expositions of the Buddha's teachings. Without them, these talks would not have happened, and this book would not be possible.

A very special thank-you to my friends whose continued understanding and generosity have supported my work and the publication of this book. Those who typed the manuscript from tapes made during the talks have given freely of their time, energy, and love to the propagation of the Dhamma.

May everyone connected with this joint undertaking reap the excellent karma caused by their gift. May this book contribute to happiness and joy in the hearts of its readers.

Ayya Khema
Buddha-Haus, Germany
December, 1995

Opening the Heart and Mind

❧

1

Taking Refuge
A Kind of Love Affair

ॐ *T*aking refuge in the Enlightened One *(Buddha)*, the teaching *(Dhamma)*, and the community of enlightened disciples *(Sangha)* has a deep significance. A refuge is a shelter, a safe place. There are very few safe places in this world. In fact, to find a totally safe shelter anywhere in worldly life is impossible. Physical shelters burn down, get demolished, disappear. Buddha-Dhamma-Sangha is not a physical shelter but a spiritual one, a haven protected from the storm. On the ocean the storms, winds, and waves make progress difficult. When a ship finally reaches the shelter of a harbor, where the water is calm, it can come to anchor. This is what it means to take refuge in Buddha-Dhamma-Sangha.

We feel that we have finally found the place where we can come to rest: the teaching that promises, without a shadow of a doubt, that there is an end to suffering, to all the ills besetting mankind. The teaching, the Dhamma propounded by the great teacher and perpetuated by his Sangha, shows us the way. "Sangha" here means those who become enlightened through the Buddha's teaching, not necessarily those who wear robes. When we accept that promise by realizing the possibility of an end to suffering and by trusting in the Dhamma's efficacy, taking refuge is very meaningful.

Buddhaṁ saraṇaṁ gacchāmi	To the Buddha I go for refuge.
Dhammaṁ saraṇaṁ gacchāmi	To the Dhamma I go for refuge.
Saṅghaṁ saraṇaṁ gacchāmi	To the Sangha I go for refuge.

It is essential to understand the meaning of the Pali. Otherwise we are repeating words in a foreign language just like parrots, who don't know what they are saying.

When we feel that taking refuge is a reality for us, our hearts open up in devotion, gratitude, and respect toward Buddha-Dhamma-Sangha. We feel grateful that cessation of suffering is available; we feel devotion to the path, which promises an otherworldly reality; we feel appreciative of those who made propagating the path their life's work.

Taking refuge can become the most important thing in our lives. Everything that we do can be done for Buddha-Dhamma-Sangha. I can carry stones for Buddha-Dhamma-Sangha, and they weigh nothing. But if I carry stones because somebody tells me to carry stones, they're heavy and the work is tiring. It is not difficult at all to perform tasks for the highest ideal that promises another level of being once we have seen that the reality in which humanity lives is unsatisfactory and are willing to let go of it.

Most of us gladly take refuge—with utter devotion, gratitude, and respect—in someone who has reached the most elevated consciousness possible and is able and willing to explain the path in such a way that we can actually follow it.

When we feel gratitude, devotion, and respect, we have love in our hearts. Love and respect go hand in hand with the spiritual path. These two feelings are appropriate and essential for any relationship we may have, but even more so for the spiritual path, which is the closest relationship we can have because it concerns our own being. Heart and mind must both be engaged. The mind understands and the heart loves, and unless that fusion happens, we may limp along on one leg. The integration of intellect and emotion helps us walk ahead steadily.

Unsteadiness in our practice will again and again bring dissatisfaction into our hearts and also skeptical doubt: Am I doing the right thing? What's this all about? Why don't I do what everybody else is doing? Skeptical doubt arises because a lack of emotional connection to our practice leaves us shaky. We need to be solidly grounded and have both heart and mind wholeheartedly involved in all our actions.

In this human world we are beset by troubles, difficulties, and constant fears for ourselves and our loved ones. Finding a refuge, a safe place within all that anxiety, is so rare and valuable that most people cannot fathom its importance.

We call Buddha-Dhamma-Sangha the Three Jewels, or the Triple Gem (*Tiratana*), because they are of the utmost value. The jewels are not the physical bodies of the Buddha and the Sangha but the transcendence that they represent, the *nibbānic* consciousness, overriding all human desires and foibles.

Being able to take refuge is not only rare but denotes excellent karma. But such a wonderful opportunity will bear fruit only if we take refuge with our hearts and not just with our mouths.

All of us have at least once in our lives been in love, and we can remember the feeling, especially if the love was reciprocated. It felt marvelous, didn't it? The same exhilarating emotion can be ours if we love Buddha-Dhamma-Sangha, because we meet all three within our hearts. This can be a perpetual love affair, and whatever we do, we do for the ones we love, which becomes an easy task. Energy becomes natural and doesn't have to be aroused over and over. It arises from certainty and direction, from a heart fully connected to all we do.

The Buddha promised that we can come to the end of every bit of suffering that ever was in our hearts, and that we can reach the end of all anxiety, fear, and worry, the end of even the smallest niggling feeling that something isn't right. When we enter the path leading to the final elimination of all *dukkha* (suffering), we enter a relationship that can purify us totally and that will eventually make us part of the Enlightened Sangha. If taking refuge is understood in this way, we derive great benefit from it.

The same chants that encourage gratitude, devotion, and respect also help us memorize the teaching, leading us thereby to wisdom and insight. Here I give the English translation of the Pali original.

Homage to the Buddha:
Indeed the Blessed One is thus:
The accomplished destroyer of defilements,
A Buddha perfected by himself,
Complete in clear knowledge and compassionate conduct,
Supremely good in presence and in destiny,
Knower of the worlds,
Incomparable master of those to be tamed,
Teacher of devas and humans,

Awakened and awakener,
And the Lord by skillful means apportioning Dhamma.

Homage to the Dhamma:
The Dhamma of the Blessed One is perfectly expounded,
To be seen here and now,
Not a matter of time,
Inviting one to come and see,
Leading inward,
To be known by the wise each individually.

Homage to the Sangha:
The Sangha of the Blessed One's disciples has entered on the good way.
The Sangha of the Blessed One's disciples has entered on
the straight way.
The Sangha of the Blessed One's disciples has entered on the true way.
The Sangha of the Blessed One's disciples has entered on
the proper way.
That is to say:
The four pairs of humans, the eight types of persons,
This Sangha of the Blessed One's disciples is fit for gifts,
Fit for hospitality, fit for offerings, and fit for reverential salutation,
As the incomparable field of merit for the world.

Wisdom has three stages. The first one is knowledge acquired by hearing or reading. We reach the second stage when we make this knowledge our own by taking its guidelines to heart and trying to actualize them through thought, speech, and action. As we do this more and more, our thoughts, words, and deeds are purified, and the third and highest stage of wisdom arises.

We have all seen statues or pictures of the Buddha. Nobody knows what the Buddha really looked like, for in those days there were no cameras, and no drawings of the Buddha were made either. The statues and pictures we see depict each artist's idea of beauty and compassion.

We can make our own Buddha statue in our minds, according to how we visualize perfection and beauty. We can let golden rays emanate from it, make it the most wonderful thing we can possibly imagine, and carry it around in our hearts. This will develop love for ourselves and also help us to love others, since we see that they might be carrying the same beautiful statue around in their hearts. Even if they speak differently and look different from us, they still carry the same beauty in their hearts.

Unless we practice loving feelings toward everyone we meet, day in, day out, we're missing out on the most joyous part of life. If we can actually open our hearts, there's no difficulty in being happy. Anyone who has a successful love affair has a happy heart.

When we love the Three Jewels it is the kind of love affair that cannot disappoint us. Our lover does not run away or pick someone else. And since we haven't yet discovered the depth and profundity of the loved one, new horizons open up all the time. When we become enlightened, the whole consciousness of our beloved, the Buddha-Dhamma-Sangha, will be available to us, and we cannot possibly be disappointed.

This is a kind of transcendental relationship, not dependent upon a human being who will eventually die and who is imperfect. It is a relationship with perfection itself, which is difficult to find in the human or any other realm. We are extremely privileged to have that opportunity. Yet we must also turn our perception toward our imperfect inner reality and recognize clearly what the Three Jewels mean for us. Then loving devotion will arise and fill us. When we see the greatest beauty and purity, the greatest wisdom, we cannot help but love their expression.

We have a lot to be grateful for, and it is our own good karma that has made it possible to be here at this moment. The Dhamma protects the Dhamma practitioner. We are protected because our reactions are dependable and we have found the pathway to freedom. This is the only safety we can find.

2

The Dhamma of the Blessed One

The Dhamma of the Blessed One is perfectly expounded,
To be seen here and now
Not a matter of time,
Inviting one to come and see,
Leading inward,
To be known by the wise, each individually.

*T*he first line of this chant proclaims real faith in the Dhamma—not a belief in everything without inquiry, but an inner relationship of trust. When we are faithful to someone, we trust that person, we put ourselves in his or her hands, we have a deep connection and an inner opening. When we have faith in the teaching of the Buddha, this is all the more true. Those aspects of the Dhamma that we do not understand we leave in abeyance, but that does not shake our faith and trust.

Dhamma is the truth expounded by the Enlightened One, the law of nature surrounding us and imbedded within us. If we feel that it is "perfectly expounded," then we are very fortunate, for we have found one thing in this universe that is perfect. There is nothing else to be found that is without blemish, nor is there anything that approaches such perfection. If we have that trust, faithfulness, and love for the Dhamma and believe it to be perfectly expounded, then we have found something beyond compare. We are blessed with an inner wealth.

"To be seen here and now" means that understanding the Dhamma is up to each one of us. The Dhamma has been made clear by the Enlightened One, who taught it out of compassion, but we have to see it ourselves with an inner vision.

"Here and now" means never forgetting the Dhamma, but being aware of it in each moment. This awareness helps us to watch our reactions before they result in unskillful words or actions. When we see the positive within us, we cultivate it; when we see the negative, we substitute the positive. When we believe all our thoughts and claim justification for them, we are not seeing the Dhamma. There are no justifications, only the arising and ceasing of phenomena.

"Not a matter of time" means that we do not depend upon a buddha being alive in order to practice the Dhamma. Some people think there has to be a perfect teacher or perfect meditation. None of that is true. Mental and physical phenomena *(dhammas)* are constantly coming and going, changing without pause. When we hang on to them and consider them ours, we will believe any story our mind tells us, without discrimination. We consist of body, feelings, perceptions, mental formations, and consciousness, which we grip tightly and believe to be "me" and "mine." We need to take a step back and be a neutral observer of the whole process.

"Inviting one to come and see, leading inward": the understanding of the Dhamma leads us into our inner depth. We are not invited to come and see a meditation hall or a Buddha statue, a stupa or a shrine, but to see the dhammas arising within us. The defilements as well as the purifications are to be found inside our own hearts and minds. The arising and ceasing phenomena, which are our teachers, never rest. Dhamma is being taught to us constantly. All our waking moments are Dhamma teachers, if we make them so.

Our minds are very busy, remembering, planning, hoping, or judging. We could make our body equally busy by picking up little stones and throwing them into the water all day long. But we would consider that a foolish expenditure of energy, so we direct the body toward something more useful. We need to do the same with the mind. Instead of thinking about this and that, allowing the defilements to arise, we should direct the mind toward something beneficial, such as investigating our likes and dislikes, our desires and rejections, our ideas and views.

When the mind inquires, it does not get involved in its creations. It cannot do both at the same time. As it becomes more observant, it remains objective for longer periods. That is why the Buddha taught that mindfulness is the sole means of purification. The clear and lucid observation of all arising phenomena eventually shows that there are only mind and body constantly expanding and contracting, in the same way as the universe does. Unless we become very diligent observers, we will not notice that aspect of mind and body and cannot know the Dhamma "here and now," even though we have been "invited to come and see."

"To be known by the wise, each individually" means that no one can know the Dhamma for another. We can chant, read, discuss, and listen, but unless we watch all that arises, we will not know the Dhamma by ourselves. There is only one place where the Dhamma can be known—within our inner being. It has to be a personal experience. Meditation helps. Unless we inquire into our reactions and know why we want one thing and reject another, we have not seen the Dhamma. This practice will also give us a clear perception of impermanence *(anicca)* because our desires and dislikes are constantly changing. We will see that the mind, which is thinking, and the body, which is breathing, are both unsatisfactory (dukkha).

᧞When the mind does not operate with an uplifted, transcendental awareness, it creates suffering (dukkha). Only a measureless, illumined mind is free from that. The body produces dukkha in many ways, through its inability to remain steady. Seeing this clearly will give us a strong determination to know Dhamma by ourselves.

Wisdom arises from within and comes from an understood experience. Neither knowledge nor listening can bring it about. Wisdom also means maturity, which has nothing to do with age. Sometimes life experiences may help, but not always. Wisdom is an inner knowing, which creates self-confidence. We need not look for somebody else's confirmation and goodwill; we know for ourselves with certainty.

Treading the Dhamma path is like walking a tightrope. It leads along one straight line, and every time we slip, it hurts. When we first start to walk on the tightrope we are not used to balancing. We sway all over the place, going in many directions, wherever it is most comfortable. We may feel restricted and coerced, not being allowed to live according to our natural instincts. Yet to walk on a tightrope we have to restrict ourselves through mindfulness. These restrictions may at first feel irksome, like fetters or bonds, but later they turn out to be liberating.

To have this perfect jewel of the Dhamma in our hearts, we need to be awake and aware. Then we can prove by our watchfulness that "the

Dhamma of the Blessed one is perfectly expounded." There is no worldly jewel that can match the value of the Dhamma. Each one of us can become the owner of this priceless gem. We are most fortunate to have such an opportunity. When we wake up in the morning, let this be our first thought: What good fortune it is for me to be able to practice the Dhamma.

Building a Strong Foundation

⁊

3

Views and Opinions

⟿ ***T*** he Noble Eightfold Path, which is the blueprint for getting to *nibbāna,* or enlightenment, starts out with right view. What does it mean to have right view? In the *Brahmajāla Sutta (Brahma's Net Discourse)* the Buddha lists sixty-two kinds of views, all of which are wrong because they are discolored by likes and dislikes that ego delusion has created. This is vital to remember. Views and opinions cause us to argue, to feel resentful, to get worried and fearful, to make enemies, and they can't be perfectly right until enlightenment is attained.

That doesn't mean we can't make decisions. But viewpoints and opinions are set ways of looking at things, preconceived notions about the world. We can't very well operate without them, but it is essential that we have an inner conviction that they are only viewpoints and not absolute truths. Then we can accept other people's opinions and don't have to take a final stand. We can say, "This is my viewpoint and this is somebody else's." The two might be opposed to each other, but that doesn't necessarily mean we have to get angry or argumentative and believe that only our views are correct.

Here's an example. Let's say that four friends are walking through the forest, and one of them is a botanist. He carries a notebook and pencil, and, delighted by the plants he sees, writes down their names or makes drawings so he can look them up later. Another is a forest ranger, and all he can think about is where he can set the next fire to burn the undergrowth in order to protect the forest from greater destruction. The third is a conservationist who wants to appeal to politicians to preserve this forest for future generations. The last one is a dairy farmer who mentally calculates how many trees could be cut down in order to graze more cattle. They all have their own view of what this forest means. If each of the four friends insisted that his view was the only correct one, they might not remain friends for long. Each is convinced that his own way of looking at the forest is the right way. But there are dozens of other ways of looking at a forest, and this is true of all aspects of existence. Each one of those four friends' viewpoints has merit but isn't absolute. Each is a partial view whose appeal is due to the individual's own likes or dislikes and identifications.

The Buddha's right view is *sammā diṭṭhi*. It is interesting that diṭṭhi itself—meaning "view"—denotes *wrong* view. Right view is the first step on the Noble Eightfold Path and also the culmination of all practice. As a first step it gets us onto the path, and as the last step it means insight into absolute truth. First we need to be convinced that something needs to be done—and can be done—about our inner purity, and that it isn't the fault of the world that things aren't going right. This first inkling of right view makes it possible to enter into a spiritual discipline. There are three parts to the teaching: *sīla, samādhi* and *paññā*. Sīla is moral conduct, samādhi is concentration, and paññā is wisdom. One usually considers them in that order, but the Noble Eightfold Path starts out with wisdom as our entry point.

Another aspect of right view is karma. Whatever we do, think, or say causes an effect. It may be minor and mild or it may have strong repercussions. When we have good thoughts, good speech will follow, and from good speech, good actions result. The immediate karmic results *(vipāka)* are satisfaction and contentment, which support successful meditation. To meditate with dissatisfaction and discontentment in the heart is a contradiction in terms. Meditation is meant to bring peace and happiness, but we can't really meditate until we are at least a little happy. Since only a joyful and contented mind can let go of thinking, the karma that our thoughts generate has an enormous influence on our meditation. Every time we make a choice, we're making karma, and in our waking moments we're making choices most of the time. Some are very minor, some of medium importance. Life consists of "middling" moments. It contains only a few absolute highs or lows; mostly it consists of small choices: How am I going to react in this situation? How can I answer a certain demand? How do I feel about this person? How will I handle these circumstances? What's going on in my mind? Is it useful? Profitable? Wholesome? All these choices, from morning to evening, create our karmic results. While they may not produce devastating effects, they will certainly engender mind states that are either conducive to meditation or not. We have to remember that each single choice we make is important and that it is our own decision. We mustn't ever be a slave to our emotions or bound by our reactions. Choosing makes karma.

Within the realm of our own karmic results we have only a certain amount of choice. The more skillful our decisions are, the more opportunities arise. But if we want our meditation to be successful, we have to stay alert all day, no matter what we think or do. Right view recognizes that we are the owners of our karma and that our personal views can never be absolutely right. It's all right to have them, with the proviso that they could be wrong. If we have that kind of attitude toward our views, we can get along with other people quite easily when they utter their beliefs and opinions. That's the very beginning of the path.

The path leads to absolute right view about this person called "me," who has problems, difficulties, joys, pleasures, ambitions, hopes, wishes, and memories. We eventually come to see that this person is made up of different ideas and feelings and that the right view about this person cannot be the one we entertain now, since there are too many difficulties besetting our hearts and minds. It has to be an entirely different view, if it is to bring peace to our hearts. To change our understanding of ourselves we need a calm and trained mind that can pull itself out of its old habitual patterns of viewing self.

We all have ideas about ourselves—our abilities, our attractiveness, our difficulties. These are all views, not basic and absolute truths. In the relative reality in which we live, they are more or less true. But on an absolute level, the level that underlies all that exists, none have any meaning. The only view that has absolute validity sees total changeability in all conditioned things. Everything we are is a manifestation of an ever changing body and an ever changing mind. We consist of the four great elements, and no core substance can be found. This view is not intellectually realizable, nor will the mind accept it unless meditation produces a state of peace and happiness independent of outer conditions. Only a happy mind will accept such a radically different viewpoint. A mind burdened by difficulties cannot possibly accept that there is really nobody there who is experiencing those difficulties.

There are two ways to understand the Buddha's teaching: relatively and absolutely. On a relative level, each one of us must try hard to achieve a concentrated state of mind. On an absolute level, there isn't anybody there to try. In order to reach an absolute understanding, we must use our relative reality. Unless *I* am trying, there is no way to realize absolute truth. These are two different levels of thinking and awareness. We can't absorb the higher level of consciousness unless the lower level has first been totally traversed and purified.

In the beginning right view is relative: we realize that we can change ourselves and that we can be aware of karma and its results; and we know that our views are not absolute. With the practice of the Noble Eightfold Path we eventually come to the absolute right view.

The other aspect of the Noble Eightfold Path that is also part of wisdom is right intention. It is of the utmost necessity for the spiritual path that our intentions be correct. In the beginning our intentions may be mostly self-centered. We may come to spiritual practice for the wrong reasons. That doesn't matter. It wasn't unknown even during the Buddha's lifetime. Eventually, through practice, our intentions change and adapt themselves to the Dhamma.

The Buddha had a cousin called Nanda who couldn't make up his mind whether he wanted to be a monk or get married. Because his famous cousin, the Buddha, was a monk, he was attracted to that kind of life. His personal inclinations, however, pulled him toward marriage. Finally his parents got tired of his constant indecision. They procured a wife for him and set a date for his wedding. The Buddha was the guest of honor. After the noon meal, before the wedding ceremony had started, the Buddha said to Nanda, "Come and carry my alms bowl to the monastery for me." Nanda couldn't very well refuse, as the Buddha was the most respected member of the whole clan and the guest of honor. Although he wasn't very willing, he traipsed behind the Buddha with the alms bowl. When they got to the monastery, the Buddha told him to sit down a moment. Nanda replied that he couldn't do that, he was in a hurry. The Buddha asked him why he was in such a hurry. "I'm getting married today, you know that. You were there." The Buddha asked, "Why do you want to get married? What's so important about that?" Nanda said, "This lady is so beautiful; I love her and want to marry her. But I really have to go now." The Buddha replied, "If you stay here in the monastery and practice according to my instructions, you can have five hundred women much more beautiful than she is." "Really?" asked Nanda. "Yes," replied the Buddha. So Nanda stayed and practiced. Every once in a while he would go to the Buddha and say, "Now what about those five hundred beautiful women you promised me?" And the Buddha said, "I told you that once you had practiced you would know all about that. Go and practice some more." Nanda kept on with the spiritual disciplines, became enlightened, and was no longer interested in five hundred beautiful ladies. What the Buddha had promised him was that, if he practiced well enough, he would eventually see the devas, who are far more beautiful than human women. Obviously this was a wrong intention for going to the monastery, but it was the one thing that would capture Nanda's imagination, since he was that kind of person. Through continued practice he changed his character. He didn't have the right motivation at first, but the right results followed.

Right intention has to be connected with the effort of practice, which we make both in meditation and in our daily life. These two, right view and right intention, are the first part of the path.

The Buddha compared people to four kinds of clay vessels. One type of vessel has holes in the bottom. We can pour in as much water as we like and it runs right out. When this type of person hears the Dhamma it goes in one ear and out the other. The second type of vessel has cracks. Though we pour in the Dhamma, it seeps out slowly until the vessel is empty again. The third vessel is full to the brim with stale water, which are views and opinions. One can't pour anything new in, everything is already known. The only useful vessel is the fourth, without holes or cracks and totally empty. Emptiness is not a negative state; it denotes a mind that has no tension, no worry or fear, and is wide open to see the Dhamma within.

Such a mind has let go of all preconceived ideas about the world and the people in it. If our ideas up to now have not brought total and absolute happiness, it is much better to let go of them and be an empty vessel into which the Dhamma can be poured. As the Dhamma fills us, it changes our outlook and eventually brings us to right view.

One of the ways we are enlightened is called "signless liberation." This means that we are aware that nothing has any significance; nothing is important enough to keep in the mind; everything is lacking substance. When the mind is not preoccupied, it can look at things afresh. When we look at a tree with our habitual mind states, all we see is the old, familiar concept of a tree. We never really see the living tree. Our preconceived notion of a tree may be that it is good to have trees because they supply oxygen. Or we think it is not good to have them because ants live in them. Or we appreciate trees because of their fruit. Or we might not like trees because their shade inhibits vegetable growth, but we never actually see what is there.

When the mind is empty of preconceived notions, we can see the world from a new angle. It might look quite different. Everything is constantly moving. When we ride in a train it may look as though the scenery is moving. Actually the train is moving, but we can't see that. It is the same with us now. We're actually sitting in a moving train, but it seems to us as though we are stationary. This is a total misconception. But if we look at everything around us, including ourselves, without any preconceived notions, we get nearer to absolute reality and develop right view, which becomes a personal experience. That is in conformity with the Buddha's teaching—to practice, not to believe. Only when we speak about an experience that we've had do we approach truth, no matter what the experience. So long as we talk about what we think and believe, we are merely voicing views and opinions. The more ideas we carry around with us, the less chance we have for peaceful meditation or seeing the world properly.

It's interesting to know that the eye sees only colors and forms and that the ear hears only sounds. The rest is all mind-made. There is no absolute reality corresponding to what we see and hear, yet our reactions to sense contacts dominate us. When we hear a bird sing or a dog bark, the reality is only sound. But the mind says, "Dogs barking. I wish they'd be quiet. I want to meditate." Or, "It's a good thing we haven't any dogs." Or, "I am glad cats don't bark." All these are mental reactions. When the eye sees form and color, it interprets them through perception based on memory. We grasp at that perception and think it is ours and must be correct. For example, what we see as a clock, a small child might think is a building block. This is a different explanation arising from a different level of development. My perceptions do not have to be right. They are just perceptions, and just as prone to misinterpretation as our sense contacts. The world within and the world without are not what they appear to be. Keep in mind that viewpoints are only viewpoints and that on an absolute level the whole world, including ourselves, is not what it appears to be.

4
To Control One's Mind

め Our old friend dukkha can be triggered by bodily discomfort, but more often it is caused by the mind's aberrations and convolutions. The mind creates dukkha, and that is why we must guard the mind well.

Our own mind makes us happy or unhappy—nothing else in the world can. Since events trigger reactions, often catching us unaware, we need to develop attentiveness to our own mind moments.

We have a good chance to do that in meditation. There are two directions in meditation: calm *(samatha)* and insight *(vipassanā)*. If we can achieve some calm, that indicates that concentration is improving. But unless that valuable skill is used for insight, it may be a waste of time. If the mind becomes calm, joy often arises, but we can observe how fleeting and impermanent that joy is, and how even bliss is just a passing condition. Only insight is irreversible. The deeper the calm within us, the better it will withstand disturbances. In the beginning any noise, discomfort, or thought will break it up, especially if the mind has not been calm during the day.

The impermanence (anicca) of everything needs to be seen clearly at all times, and not just during meditation. The fact of constant change should give us insight into reality. Mindfulness is the heart of Buddhist meditation and insight is its goal. We spend only some of our time in meditation, but we can use all of our time to gain insight into our own mind. That is where the whole world is happening for us. Nothing outside of what we know in the mind exists for us.

The more we watch the mind and see what it does to us and for us, the more we will be inclined to take good care of it and treat it with respect. One of the biggest mistakes we can make is taking the mind for granted.

The mind has the capacity to create good and evil for us. Only when we are able to remain happy and calm, no matter what conditions are arising, can we say that we have gained a little control. Until then we are out of control and our thoughts are our master.

> Whatever harm a foe may do to foe,
> or hater unto one he hates,
> the ill-directed mind indeed
> can do one greater harm.

> What neither mother, nor father too,
> nor any other relative can do,
> the well-directed mind indeed
> can do one greater good.
>
> *Dhammapada 42, 43*

In the Buddha's words, nothing is more valuable than a controlled and skillfully directed mind. Taming one's mind does not happen only in meditation—that is just one specific training. It can be likened to learning to play tennis. One practices with a coach, again and again, until one has found one's balance and aptitude and can actually play a match. The match in which we tame the mind is everyday life—every situation we encounter.

The greatest support we can have is mindfulness, which means being totally present in each moment. If the mind remains centered, it cannot make up stories about the injustice of the world or one's friends, or about one's desires or sorrows. All these stories could fill many volumes, but when we are mindful such verbalizations stop. Being mindful means being fully absorbed in the moment, leaving no room for anything else. We are filled with the momentary happening, whatever it is—standing or sitting or lying down, feeling pleasure or pain—and we maintain a nonjudgmental awareness, a "just knowing."

Clear comprehension implies evaluation: we comprehend the purpose of our thought, speech, or action, and we know whether we are using skillful means and whether we have actually achieved the required results. We need to gain some distance from ourselves to evaluate dispassionately, for if we are completely identified with an event, objectivity is nearly impossible.

Mindfulness coupled with clear comprehension provides us with the necessary distance.

Any dukkha that we have, great or small, continuous or intermittent, is created by our minds. We create all that happens to us, nobody else is involved. Everybody else is playing his own role in this drama called "life." Sometimes other people just happen to be around, and we imagine they are responsible for our difficulties. But in reality, whatever we do arises from our own mind moments.

The more we watch our thoughts in meditation, the more insight can arise. When we watch mind moments arising, staying, and ceasing, detachment from our thinking process results, bringing dispassion. Thoughts come and go all the time, just like the breath. If we hang on to them, problems arise. We believe we own our thoughts and have to do something about them, especially if they are negative. This is bound to create dukkha.

The Buddha's formula for the highest effort is worth remembering: "Not to let an unwholesome thought arise that has not yet arisen. Not to sustain an unwholesome thought that has already arisen. To arouse a wholesome thought that has not yet arisen. To sustain a wholesome thought that has already arisen."

The quicker we master this effort, the better it is for our well-being. This is part of the training we undergo in meditation. When we have learned to drop whatever arises in meditation, we can do the same with unwholesome thoughts in daily life. When we can abandon distracting thoughts while meditating on the breath, we can use the same skill to protect our mind at all times. The more we learn to shut our mind-door to the negativities that disturb our inner peace, the easier our life becomes. Peace of mind is not indifference. Recognizing and letting go is not suppression. A peaceful mind is a compassionate mind.

Dukkha is self-made and self-perpetuated. If we are sincere in wanting to get rid of it, we have to watch the mind carefully. We have to gain insight into what is really happening within. What triggers us? How do we react? There are innumerable triggers, but only two reactions. One is equanimity, the other craving.

We can learn from everything. Today some anagarikas had to wait quite a long time at the bank, which was an exercise in patience. Whether the exercise was successful or not does not matter. It was a learning experience.

Everything we do is an exercise and a challenge. This is our purpose as human beings, our only reason for being here. We use the time on our little planet for learning and growing. We should think of our life as an adult education class. Any other life purpose is mistaken.

We are guests here, giving a limited guest performance. If we use our time to gain insight into ourselves—our likes and dislikes, our resistances, our rejections, our worries and fears—then we are living our lives to the best advantage. It is a great skill to live in such a way. The Buddha called it "urgency" *(saṁvega),* a sense of having to work on ourselves now and not leave it for some future, unspecified date when one may have more time. Everything can be a learning experience, and the only time is now.

When we meet our old friend dukkha, we should ask, "Where did you come from?" When we get an answer, we should inquire again, and go deeper. There is only one true answer, but we will not find it immediately. We have to go through several answers until we get to the bottom line, which is ego. When we reach this point, we know we have come to the end of the questioning and to the beginning of insight. We can then try to see how the ego has produced dukkha again. What did we do, how did we react? When we see the cause, we may be able to let go of that particular wrong view. Having seen cause and effect for ourselves, we do not forget them. Single drops fill a bucket, little by little we purify. Every moment is worthwhile.

The more we experience every moment as worthy of our attention, the more energy is generated in the mind. There are no useless moments, every single one is important if we use it skillfully. Then strength of mind arises. Single moments add up to a life that is lived in the best possible way.

5

Ignorance

ﾐ *I*gnorance doesn't mean that we don't know our ABCs. Ignorance in Buddhist terminology means one thing only—that we're ignoring the Four Noble Truths. Ignorance is the beginning of the wheel of birth and death *(saṁsāra),* which turns again and again. The Four Noble Truths are the core or kernel of the Buddha's teaching. If we ignore them, we ignore the essence.

We may have picked out a few bits and pieces of the teaching that we find palatable and not too terribly difficult. Maybe we enjoy hearing about becoming enlightened. Or we like the fact that it isn't necessary to react when someone speaks to us nastily. Or maybe we are hoping to experience bliss if we meditate long enough. Or we appreciate loving-kindness, helpfulness, and generosity. Certainly these are all things the Buddha has taught. But when we ignore the core teachings, it is as if we are circumambulating the outer edges of the Buddha's edifice. This widely shared habit dilutes the potency of the teaching. Nibbling at the outer edges of the teaching leaves us with a feeling of uncertainty. We begin to doubt whether we should continue to meditate and practice or instead find a more pleasant and comfortable lifestyle.

The kernel and substance of life, such as we know it in the human realm, is unsatisfactoriness (dukkha). There is no fulfillment in life; on the contrary, life is constantly beset with difficulties of body and mind. Being born is dukkha, actually a new beginning of all dukkha. If our personal experiences have not yet brought us peace and fulfillment within, then what is our alternative? What pathway is open to us?

The Buddha's answer is the "deathless," or nibbāna, which includes no more rebirth. Should we aim to be born in a better state next time with more money, more friends, better health, more wisdom? Is that the answer? Or are we hoping to be born in the deva realms? Some people think that must be the answer. They believe that the grass is always greener on the other side of the fence. Maybe it is. Certain features of those realms are appealing. But if we know for a fact that birth is dukkha, then we also know that birth in any realm is dukkha.

How can something be deathless? Nibbāna can be because there is no further birth in it, and where there is no birth there can be no death. If there is such a thing as the deathless, and if we recognize that birth is dukkha, then what is left to us other than the path toward the deathless? It is not enough to try meditation tentatively, hoping for some bliss and to learn some of the Buddha's teaching to improve our interaction with others. It is enough only when the heart says, "There are no other choices but to attain the deathless."

One certain way of reaching that conviction is having sufficient dukkha. Of course, nobody would wish that for anyone else, but the experience of much suffering is often enough to turn the tide. There are many stories from the Buddha's lifetime when women in particular were experiencing so much dukkha, losing their families and loved ones, that they had no other choices left. In our society there may be too many alternatives left. We could conceivably go to the beach and enjoy the ocean, or we could take a trip to India or the Riviera, or start a new friendship, or go out to eat Chinese food. If we look at any of the alternatives we can conjure up, we recognize each one of them as a sense contact—which is always short lived. Unless that becomes entirely clear, our spiritual growth will always be shaky. There's a Zen saying, "When you walk, walk. When you run, run. But for heaven's sake don't wobble." Whatever we do on this path, let's really walk, steadily and resolutely.

The only alternatives to enlightenment are sense contacts. Many of the Buddha's exhortations are about the dangers of sensual desires. We should check to see whether that's true or whether the Buddha is just telling us interesting stories that we haven't read anywhere else. The path exists only inside ourselves. The Dhamma can never be alive in a book or in some-body's words; it has to come alive in ourselves. We must investigate whether it's true that all pleasures come from sense contacts and all our displeasures from either lacking them or from contacting something we don't like.

We have two choices. We can have pleasurable sense contacts or we can have the solidity of the path that leads out of birth, decay, aging, and death—out of all dukkha. Interestingly, only very few people choose the latter. Dukkha is one way of preparing oneself to choose the solidity of the path and commit to practice.

We need courage to choose the way of the Dhamma. If we take the path leading out of dukkha, we have to leave a lot of attachments and support systems behind. That takes courage. We discard much of that which we once believed to bring fulfillment and happiness. We need courage to break with that and begin to stand alone. That doesn't mean that we become unpleasant to our former friends or tell our families we never want to see them again. We begin to loosen our attachments, our clinging and belonging. We recognize beyond any doubt that there is nothing more important to be done than treading the path to enlightenment. Then all our energies and priorities are geared to this objective.

Success can come only if we are one-pointed in our efforts. Then all our experiences—pleasant, unpleasant, or neutral—are part of the Dhamma and considered a training. If an unpleasant feeling arises we know immediately, "This is an unpleasant feeling and I'm reacting to it, but I don't have to do that. I can also drop the reaction." If our priorities are still with sense contacts, this won't work. We can't have the Noble Eightfold Path plus sense desires, all in one nice package deal. On the contrary, the Noble Eightfold Path probably provides quite a few unpleasant sense contacts because it requires self-discipline and self-control, which often result in physical discomfort.

We also cannot expect success immediately. But we know where we are going. Once we know our direction and no longer need to make choices or worry about guidance, a feeling of security arises. We can lean on the excellent authority of the Buddha, and we don't need to determine our way to spiritual awakening. We have a sure guideline upon which to base our lives.

One of our great difficulties can be to find out what is right for this person called "me." Where does our specialness lie? There are five *khandhas*—the body and the four parts of mind. There are the four elements and the thirty-two parts of the body. There is nothing and nobody special—

everybody's the same. We don't have to find out what's right for each of us. All we have to do is make a choice between pleasant sense contacts and the end of dukkha. That one choice determines our lives.

If we no longer ignore the Four Noble Truths but take them as the core of our life, then our ignorance abates somewhat. It vanishes completely only when the Third Noble Truth has been manifested—that is, when we attain liberation, nibbāna, the cessation of all dukkha. Until then, we can at least diminish ignorance by no longer ignoring its root cause, our identification with the "I."

All the different teachings of the Buddha assist us in staying on the path. In one of his discourses Venerable Sāriputta enumerates a number of ways of cultivating right view that help us to increase our own understanding. Most important of all, we need to investigate our motives for speaking, thinking, and acting the way we do. When our relationships don't flow smoothly, when they don't mix effortlessly like milk with water, we need to look at our motivations. It's not the other person's problems that we need to find but our own. Motives are like icebergs—one-third visible and two-thirds hidden. Unless we can learn to see ourselves more deeply, we can't recognize our ego-dominated activities. We need to examine our motives for purity: Are they for the benefit of others or for ourselves? Are they rooted in self-affirmation or fear? We have to check our intentions because we all make our own karma. As one of the five daily recollections states: "I am the owner of my karma, heir to my karma."

The foundation of our moral conduct rests on right speech, right action, and right livelihood. Without these as an unwavering guide, all personal power dissipates. Our strength does not lie in the body but in inner security, which arises only if we know ourselves to be blameless. Trying to lean on others brings weakness, which is dangerous. Others are just as impermanent as we are. Mothers, fathers, husbands, wives, teachers—all depart, die, change their minds, or are not around when we need them. We need to be a good guardian of ourselves, watching our steps carefully.

Right effort, right concentration, and right mindfulness need to be firmly anchored within. Right effort means applying ourselves steadily, over and over again, not only in meditation but during all our waking moments. If we haven't learned or understood something new, or haven't extended some help or love, our day is wasted. Days are precious, and each one is the only one we have. The past is gone, and the future is conjecture. The next airplane may crash, the next bus might topple over. This is the hour for practice. Just because we have survived in the past is no guarantee we will continue to do so. Unless we use each day to the full, gaining greater insight into ourselves and the teaching, our effort is not right. Right effort becomes a habit that all of us can develop to good advantage.

Having right mindfulness every single moment is an ideal that we may not be able to actualize just yet. But unless we have the determination to increase our mindfulness from moment to moment, we will easily forget to practice it. Mindfulness is not just a word or a discourse by the Buddha, but a meaningful state of mind. It means we have to be here now, in this very moment, and we have to know what is happening internally and externally. It means being alert to our motives and learning to change unwholesome thoughts and emotions into wholesome ones. Mindfulness is a mental activity that in due course eliminates all suffering. It shows us clearly that there is nothing else happening except the movement of the five khandhas—body, sense consciousness, feelings, perceptions, and mental formations. In the beginning mindfulness takes away worries and fears about past and future and keeps us anchored in the present. In the end it points to right view of the self.

As far as right concentration goes, all we can do is try our best. One part of concentration is renunciation, letting go of pleasant sights and sounds, nice odors, tastes, sensations, and thoughts. We're usually very fond of these sense contacts and cling to them fiercely. We also need to have sufficient self-confidence in our ability to meditate. We need to reach for that which we consider difficult and make it possible.

Inner readiness is needed to regard the Four Noble Truths and the Noble Eightfold Path as the main focus of our lives and everything else as circumstantial. If we have more than an academic interest in the Buddha's teaching, we will want to live by these truths, which are a one-way street to nibbāna.

6
Dukkha for Knowledge and Vision

The "twelve-point dependent origination" *(paṭiccasamuppāda)* starts with ignorance *(avijjā),* goes through karma formations *(sankhāra),* rebirth consciousness, mind and matter, sense contacts, feeling, craving, clinging, becoming, birth, and ends with death. Being born means dying. During that sequence there is one point of escape: between feeling and craving. This is called mundane *(lokiya)* dependent origination.

The Buddha also taught a supermundane, transcendental *(lokuttara)* series of causes and effects. It starts with unsatisfactoriness (dukkha), with an awareness and inner knowledge of the inescapable suffering in the human realm. Dukkha needs to be seen for what it really is, namely, the starting point of our spiritual journey. Unless we know and see dukkha, we have little reason to practice. If we have not acknowledged the overall existence of dukkha, we won't be interested in getting out of its clutches.

When we do acknowledge dukkha, we no longer try to find a way out through human endeavor. We will not try to become richer or more knowledgeable or to own more or to have more friends. Seeing dukkha as an inescapable condition bound up with existence, we no longer feel oppressed by it. We accept thunder and lightning as inescapable—understanding that there have to be thunder, lightning, and rain so we can grow food—so we do not reject them. Dukkha is equally inescapable. Without it, the human condition would not exist. There would be no rebirth, decay, and death. If we understand this, we lose our resistance. The moment we are no longer repelled by dukkha, we suffer much less. Resistance creates a craving to get rid of dukkha, which only intensifies it.

Having understood dukkha, we may be fortunate enough to make contact with the true Dhamma, the Buddha's teaching. This is due to our good karma. There are innumerable people who never get in touch with the Dhamma. They might even be born in a place where the Dhamma is being taught, but they will have no opportunity to hear it. There are many more people who will not be searching for the Dhamma because they are still looking for some escape route in the human realm, which is the wrong direction. Those who have seen that the world will not provide real happiness still need good karma to be able to listen to true Dhamma. If these conditions arise, then faith results.

Faith has to be based on trust and confidence. If these are lacking, the path will not open. We become trusting, like a child holding the hand of a grown-up when crossing the street. The child believes that the grown-up will be watching out for traffic so that no accident will happen. The small child does not have the capacity to gauge when it is safe to cross, but it trusts someone with greater experience.

We are like children compared to the Buddha. If we have a childlike innocence, we can give ourselves unstintingly to the teaching and the practice, holding the hand of the true Dhamma that will guide us. Life and practice are simplified when we no longer judge and choose: "I should go somewhere else to find out how others do it." Weighing all the possibilities is not conducive to good practice or to getting out of dukkha. Trust in the Dhamma helps to keep the mind steady. We have to find out for ourselves if this is the correct escape route. If we do not try, we will not know.

If we persist in regarding dukkha as a calamity, we will not have enough space in the mind to trust. We will be full of grief and pain, and we will forget that all of us experience our karmic results and nothing else. This is part of being a human being, subject to our own karma.

The understanding of dukkha has to be firm to arouse trust in that part of the teaching that we have not yet experienced ourselves. Such trust brings joy, without which the path is a heavy burden. An essential ingredient of the spiritual life, joy is not to be mistaken for pleasure, exhilaration, or exuberance. Joy is a feeling of ease and gladness, knowing we have found a way that transcends all suffering. People sometimes have the mistaken idea that being holy or pious means having a sad face and walking around in a mournful way. Yet the Buddha is said never to have cried and is usually depicted with a half-smile on his face. "Holiness" does not mean sadness but rather "wholeness." Without joy there can be no wholeness. Inner joy carries with it the certainty that the path is blameless, the practice fruitful, and the conduct appropriate.

We need to sit down to meditate with a joyous feeling. Then the whole experience of meditation will culminate in happiness. This brings us tranquility, for we no longer look around for outside satisfaction but only into ourselves. There is nowhere to go and nothing to do, it is all happening within. Such tranquility creates the feeling of being in the right spot at the right time. It creates ease of mind and is conducive to eliminating skeptical doubt *(vicikicchā)*.

Tranquility helps concentration to arise. Dukkha itself can lead us to proper concentration if we understand it properly. We must not reject it, take it to be a quirk of fate, or blame other people for causing it. Right concentration makes it possible for the mind to stretch. The mind that is limited, obstructed, and defiled cannot grasp the profundity of the teaching. It may get an inkling that there is something extraordinary available, but it cannot go deep. Only a concentrated mind can.

A concentrated mind may then experience "knowledge and vision of things as they really are" *(yathā-bhūta-ñānadassana)*, a phrase that the Buddha often used to describe a kind of seeing that is distinct from seeing things as we think they are or as we want them to be—comfortable and pleasant. Until now, we have gained a clear perception of our dislikes mainly when events have failed to support our ego belief, when we got what we did *not* want. In knowing and seeing things as they really are, we reach a deeper view. We come to see that within this realm of impermanence, unsatisfactoriness, and corelessness (anicca, dukkha, anattā), *nothing* can be grasped and found to be solid and satisfying. No person, no possession, no thought, no feeling. Nothing can be clung to and found to be steady and supportive.

This is right view, beyond our ordinary, everyday perception. It results from right concentration and comes from dealing with dukkha in a positive, welcoming way. When we try to escape from dukkha by either forgetting about it, running away from it, blaming it on someone else, becoming depressed by it, or feeling sorry for ourselves, we are creating more dukkha. All these methods are based on self-delusion. The "knowledge and vision of things as they really are" is the first step on the Noble Path of insight; everything else has been the preliminary work.

Sometimes our understanding may feel like one of those mystery pictures that children play with. Now you see it, now you don't. When any aspect of Dhamma is clearly visible to us, we must keep returning to that vision. If it is correct, dukkha has no sting, it just is. Decay, disease, and death do not appear fearful. There is nothing to fear because everything falls apart continually. This body disintegrates, and the mind changes every moment.

Without knowledge and vision of reality, the practice is difficult. But after having this clear perception, the practice remains the only possible thing to do. Everything else is only tangential and a distraction. From such knowledge arises disenchantment with what the world has to offer. All the glitter turns out to be worthless fool's gold, which gives us pleasure one moment and displeasure the next. The world of the senses has so often fooled us, yet we remain enmeshed in it out of habit. And we will continue to experience dukkha until the true vision arises.

There is a poster available in Australia that reads: "Life: Be in It." Would it not be better if it said, "Life: Be out of It"? Life and existence are bound up with the constant renewal of our sense contacts—seeing, hearing, tasting, touching, smelling, and thinking. Only when we have clear perception will disenchantment set in, and then even the most wonderful sense contact will no longer entice us. Māra, the tempter, loses his grip, and we show him the door. He waits at the doorstep to slip in again at the first possible opportunity, of course, but he will never again be so comfortably ensconced within us.

This clear perception brings a great deal of security and satisfaction to the heart. One will not be swayed to leave the path of practice. So long as Māra beckons, there can be no peace in the heart. We cannot be at ease and satisfied because something new always tempts us. With knowledge and vision of things as they really are and subsequent disenchantment, we realize that the Buddha's path leads us to tranquility, peace, and the end of dukkha.

Dukkha is really our staunchest friend, our most faithful supporter. We will never find another friend or helpmate like it, if we see it correctly, without resistance or rejection. When we use dukkha as our incentive for practice, gratitude and appreciation for it arise. This takes the sting out of our pain and transforms it into our most valuable experience.

7
Malleable Mind

~ In the Buddha's discourses it is often said that "the mind should become pliable, malleable, wieldy, and steadfast." How can a mind attain these attributes? The ordinary, untrained mind has a quality of stickiness. It keeps on remembering old hurts and resentments, comparing the past to the present, and hanging on to its dissatisfactions. We believe all the thoughts and projections that fill our minds. A mind like ours seems to have a fence around it, and within that enclosure all understanding takes place.

How recently have we thought something entirely new, something that has never entered our minds before? When was the last time we had an insight into universal truth? Without such breakthroughs the mind is like a needle stuck in the groove of a record, playing the same sound over and over again.

When the mind becomes concentrated and stops thinking, one can begin to experience its purity. Now the mind can be molded into a different shape instead of hardening into old patterns. Only when we experience something entirely new do we understand that the mind has the capacity to think differently.

We should be cautious about the thoughts we think during the day, because they have no true foundation; they are ego-based projections of our desires and habits. They do not touch upon absolute reality. This doesn't mean that we can abandon them right away, but we treat them with caution. They're simply old habits, not commendable in themselves, not conducive to peace and happiness.

When we become more aware of the contents of our thoughts, we also experience a new way of confronting what we hear, see, or touch—we have a kind of childlike wonder, but tempered with the wisdom of an adult. Children do not have the pure wisdom that we sometimes imagine they have, but they do perceive things in a direct, unadulterated way. Once we have become adults, we may still be able to perceive things the way a child does, as if we had never heard, seen, tasted, touched, or thought anything ever before. With a totally new understanding of our sense contacts, we can actually see reality as it is—for a moment.

When we are alert and attentive, we see that our habit-ridden minds are immature and child*ish*, not child*like*. We also see that the mind has the ability to become pliable, wieldy, and malleable, and so we recognize our inner pathway.

The Buddha compared the mind to gold. When it is found in its raw state, gold has five other metals in it. Those impurities make it brittle, so before the goldsmith can work with it he must heat the gold and melt out those five impurities. Then he has a pliable substance that he can fashion into any kind of ornament. The Buddha used this simile for the five hindrances in the mind: sensual desire, ill will, sloth and torpor, restlessness and worry, and skeptical doubt.

Our mind can bring us enlightenment, but only after it has rid itself of those hindrances and become like pure gold. Then we can experience total ease and harmony within ourselves and with the world around us.

The meditation process will enable us to experience utterly different levels of consciousness from our ordinary mind states. The idea of nonself is far removed from all the ideas we usually have. If we hear about it often enough, we'll accept it on probation, but nothing much will happen within unless we really practice. If we were to confront whatever arises as if we'd never seen or heard it before, then—only for one moment, and only if the mind is deeply concentrated—the old patterns vanish.

Unless we attain that kind of new consciousness, we're going to be in the same rut for the rest of this life. It's always going to be "me and what I want" and "me and what I don't want." This needy view is too limited for peace and happiness. How small this "me" is! It is not even the size of a pinhead when we consider the universe. Keeping that in mind shrinks the self's significance.

Whenever we have a brand new idea, something we've never thought before, a small expansion takes place. Something new like that we call an insight. If this idea does not influence our actions or reactions, however, we have not truly recognized its meaning and have understood it only intellectually.

An expansive mind sees everything within a universal context without personal identification. Suffering, impermanence, and corelessness are all universal, as are craving and its resulting manifestations. When we remember this, the particulars of our own experiences no longer have the same significance. The universality of all existence and the relative reality in which we live need to touch our hearts and minds. Until they do so—until we recognize and change our patterns of thinking and reacting—we can't enter new worlds of experience.

A malleable mind is pliable, moves freely, and embraces everything. Whenever we notice some inner change in ourselves, we need to recollect it repeatedly so as to make it second nature. One such change is becoming less concerned with comforts, belongings, ideas, hopes, and wishes. We become more and more concerned with what we can give, how we can grow, and whether we are making wholesome karma. Investigating further, we can try letting go of being a separate person for a moment and instead feeling part of all that exists. As long as we are caught within the barrier of our own minds and bodies, we cannot find true happiness. Instead we sit inside the prison of "self," waiting for someone to unlock the door. Yet we ourselves hold the key.

The hindrances keep our minds bound with iron fetters, and until we see this for ourselves no change can result. We can't wait for someone to bring us the key to our own hearts and minds. Liberation (nibbāna) and the wheel of birth and death (saṁsāra) are both to be found in our hearts. Sometimes, when we have a moment of total letting go, when we are not concerned with ourselves at all, we may even experience an inkling of what nibbāna means: a moment when the "I" is not important, when there is no particular thought pattern in the mind, when there is just awareness and no desire. Perhaps we can actually know that the "I" is not what it appears to be and let it go.

Giving oneself completely is difficult for most of us, because we think we are losing ourselves. Actually we gain everything—all spiritual teachings are agreed on that. Whatever we use as our personal identity constitutes our prison. Letting go is freedom. When we do experience a moment of letting go, we mistakenly think that it was due to a certain situation or person. But in reality we experience freedom whenever we let go of what we're clinging to. Giving in and giving up are tiny lights at the end of the tunnel that let us know freedom is possible.

Nibbāna and saṁsāra are to be found in our minds and hearts. Saṁsāra exists because of ego-consciousness and nibbāna, true happiness, arises when that is eliminated. Nothing else in the world—material possessions, attention and affirmation, appreciation, praise, knowledge, and fame—will bring total peace and freedom.

Living in the World

8

Harmonious Living

*W*hen we chant together there has to be rhythm and harmony in it. We must pay attention to timing and to other people or we will be out of tune. The same is true when we live together. We have to pay attention to others, feel our togetherness, and create harmony. People need that as a foundation for skillful living.

Skillful living often breaks down because we have, each of us, no harmony, no attention to our timing. And what we create in the world becomes a mirror image of what we find in ourselves.

The very first step in creating harmony happens within ourselves. It requires no special situation, but can be done whether we sit in the meditation hall, paddle a boat, cook lunch, read a book, or work in the garden. Creating a harmonious feeling in ourselves is dependent upon being contented. Otherwise, there is disharmony.

Contentment must not be dependent on outer conditions, which are never perfect. After months of dry weather, everyone complained about having to water too many plants. Now we have the reverse—it is too wet and the ground is muddy and slippery. Where can we find perfection in the world?

If we're looking for outer conditions to bring us contentment, we're looking in vain. We have to find inner conditions conducive to contentment. One of them is independence—not financial independence, which may bring other hazards, but emotional independence from the approval of others. This entails knowing that we are trying to do the best we can, and if someone disapproves, that's just the way things are. Not everyone approved of the Buddha either, but the Buddha said, "I do not quarrel with the world. The world quarrels with me." He accepted the fact that people would voice objections to him or his doctrine. He fully realized that not everybody can agree.

To be independent also includes not looking for support from others. Sometimes the best we can do may be very good, sometimes it is only mediocre. That too has to be accepted. We can't wait for everyone to support us. If we sometimes cannot do as well as we thought we could, that is also all right and no reason for discontent.

Emotional independence requires having a loving heart. If we are looking for love, we are emotionally dependent and often discontent because we don't get what we want, or don't get enough of it. Even if we do get enough, we still cannot count on it to fill our needs. To look for love is a totally unsatisfactory and unfulfilling endeavor. What does work, however, is loving others, which brings emotional independence and contentment. Loving others is possible whether the other person reciprocates or not. Love has nothing to do with the other, but is a quality of our own hearts.

Contentment is dependent upon creating a field of harmony within our hearts—a beautiful, open field, full of flowers, containing love, emotional independence, and self-acceptance. We do not seek love or approval but instead give them unstintingly. It's simple and it works. This constitutes a generous heart. Usually when somebody wants something from us, our ego feels threatened and fears being diminished. This is very evident on a material level, when we fear losing our possessions. We may feel the same threat when somebody wants our love. If we give love and approval, however, we are neither threatening nor threatened. To love is the only way we can live in harmony with ourselves.

Sometimes we don't feel well physically. That too is no reason for discontentment. "I am of the nature to be diseased," the Buddha asked us to recollect. There is no mention of becoming unhappy and discontent because of that. It's the nature of the body to have some problems. At other times there may be desires in the mind. We can allow that, but we don't have to get involved in those desires. If we suffer from the dukkha that mind and body generate, there will never be any contentment. Where can we find contentment? Certainly not in buildings, nature, or other people. It has only one resting place: within our own hearts. At its base lies the understanding that the gift of love and approval creates a field of harmony around us, which is also our training field.

It is a training field for skillful living because we confront ourselves in others. We need the reflection of our own being in others in order to see ourselves clearly. When there is disharmony with another person, it is a mirror image of ourselves. There can be no disharmony with others if we feel harmonious within ourselves. A mirror image does not lie. One of the Buddha's discourses describes three monks who lived together like milk and water. Their ideas and wishes merged completely. There was total harmony because none of them wanted his own way. At least this gives us an idea of what is possible, otherwise we would continue to believe that our negativity is justified.

"Harmony" has many different meanings. Mainly it is the essential core of living happily. Sometimes we get attached to our own dukkha. That's quite common, but when we see the folly of it, we can stop. Happiness is really what every living being aims for, not only human beings. We try to meditate to become happier, but we cannot sit in meditation all day long. Sometimes it even feels as though meditation brings up buried resentments and hurts, which we don't particularly want to see. It might feel as though meditation brings more dukkha than we had before, but that is only because we have finally admitted it and seen it clearly. This arouses compassion for everybody, for we see that being a human means suffering. There are different stages of spiritual development, and at the start we are like children. Whether we are in fifth, sixth, or seventh grade, we are all still children in the process of growth.

Some people are able to deal with their dukkha better than others. One unskillful way of dealing with it is trying to run away from it. When we run, dukkha has a habit of coming along. Dukkha doesn't live in a certain place or a particular situation, it lives in our own hearts. It rides on the same airplane, boat, or car with us and goes wherever we go. Trying to escape from it by running away is clearly impossible.

Another unskillful way that we have all tried is blaming some other person, situation, or thing. That means that we do not accept responsibility for our own lives. A third unskillful way of handling dukkha is becoming depressed and unhappy about it. That's our most common reaction. Then resignation follows until something nice comes along to release us— a birthday cake, ice cream, or praise—and our mood lifts.

These ways of dealing with dukkha keep us on the seesaw of desire and rejection. The only really skillful way of dealing with dukkha is to look at it as a learning experience and remember that the Buddha teaches dukkha as the first of the Four Noble Truths. Obviously he knew humanity's difficulties.

The second Noble Truth is the cause of dukkha, which is craving: wanting something that we don't have or wanting to get rid of something we do have. There are no other causes of dukkha. If we see dukkha within and don't become involved in it, but accept it as a reality, as part of life, we can also find the cause for it in ourselves. Then we can say, 'That's right, that's the way it is." If we can affirm the first and second Noble Truths, then we can assume that the third and fourth must be true as well. The third Noble Truth is the actualization of the cessation of all dukkha—nibbāna, total liberation—and the fourth is the Noble Eightfold Path leading to complete freedom. The first two truths are easy to prove—we can experience them many times each day. All we have to do is pay attention.

Dukkha arises continually and will not cease until all craving has been eliminated, when one becomes an *arahant,* fully enlightened. Why should we be surprised when dukkha arises? It would be more sensible to be surprised when dukkha doesn't arise. If we're surprised when dukkha arises, this means that we are still hoping to find total satisfaction and fulfillment in the world.

To have inner harmony we must accept dukkha as an integral part of being human. If we dislike and reject it, our resistance makes it worse, and escape from it becomes a priority. Usually that includes trying to change people, situations, our work, or whatever else comes to our minds. We can never eliminate dukkha like that, but only through the abandoning of craving—that is the Buddha's teaching. At this stage in our lives we can take his words as guidelines for practice. There already seems to be a glimmer of hope that we can verify some of the things he said, and we can take the rest on trust to try them out.

When dukkha arises, we can realize that something we want isn't happening. We can find the desire and let go of it, since there is no other way of avoiding dukkha. The more craving we abandon, the more harmony we have. Craving disrupts harmony. Imagine that we're chanting together and one person wants to be heard above all the others, or another wants to chant faster. All harmony is disrupted.

Contentment in our hearts is rooted in emotional independence, in giving love and approval rather than trying to get them. We need to realize that all dukkha depends on craving and that we must therefore let go of desires. That is the path and the teaching. We often forget these basic truths.

Why do we forget so easily? Our ego identification and affirmation is foremost and reduces everything else to unimportance. Our minds are concerned with "me" and "mine," and since everyone thinks in this way, the world is a disharmonious place. We can find harmony only in our own hearts; nobody else will hand it to us. The Buddha showed us the way through loving-kindness *(mettā)* meditation, loving-kindness conduct, meditative absorptions *(jhāna),* and insight meditation *(vipassanā).* These are all means toward liberation and not ends in themselves. Our goal is the penetration into impermanence (anicca), unsatisfactoriness (dukkha), and corelessness (anattā)—into the nature of constant change, into life's inherent difficulties, and into the games that the ego plays, disturbing peace and harmony. There are only problems when *I* am having them. If there's no "I," how can there be a problem?

Harmony is togetherness with others but also togetherness within oneself. Becoming a whole person brings harmony. The word "holy" is rooted in the word "whole." We need not be holy, just whole and complete in ourselves. It's the most difficult and the most worthwhile work we can do. When we know that there is nothing lacking in ourselves, nothing that we have to find somewhere outside, contentment and peace begin to fill our hearts.

9
Talking to One Another

~ Seeking mental solitude instead of conversation is sometimes of great benefit. The Buddha mentioned right speech many times. It is a step on the Noble Eightfold Path, one of the five precepts, and also one of the blessings in the *Mahāmaṅgala Sutta (Great Blessings Discourse)*. Kind and polite speech is mentioned there as well. There is a whole discourse that the Buddha expounded, the *Exposition of Nonconflict,* to show that speech creates conflict, if used improperly.

Most people have the idea that because they can talk they know what right speech is, which is mistaken. Right speech is a skill that has to be learned. It depends not only on our thinking processes but also on our emotional responses. When we get angry, we are certainly not likely to use right speech. If we want to feel important—an emotional aspect of our ego illusion—our speech will sound self-righteous. We need to watch not only our thoughts but our emotions as well. Only the fully enlightened, the arahant, will always use right speech. But that does not prevent us from practicing and learning as much as we can.

Speech should not be flattering or overly sweet. Such speech sounds, and is, false, but some people use it habitually. They always have an overly agreeable and exaggeratedly supportive reply. They are trying to sound kind, but it doesn't ring true.

An interesting aspect of speech, one well worth remembering, is that although speech is our main method of addressing each other, it amounts to only seven percent of our whole communication. This information comes from a woman who teaches communication workshops—that we need such workshops tells us a lot about ourselves. She has a thriving business.

People don't know how to talk to one another, especially those who live in close contact with one another. There's a lot more happening than the seven percent of communication that is verbal. Since ninety-three percent is nonverbal, we have to watch our thoughts and emotions very carefully. We cannot hide them or keep them secret. We like to believe that we can think and feel anything we like and that nobody's going to know about it, as long as we don't tell them. Nothing could be more untrue.

Thoughts and emotions are evident to anyone with even a little awareness. The feeling behind the words comes through. That's how misunderstandings arise. Somebody makes a statement that seems to him perfectly plain but the other person picks up on the feeling and hears something entirely different. The listener can of course question the speaker and the two can iron out the misunderstanding. But often people don't question, they just misunderstand, and enmity, dislike, coldness, or indifference ensue.

The feeling behind the words also shows through in our body language. If we pay attention, there's a lot we can learn from body language, facial expressions, and tone of voice. Our words and verbalizations are more limited. One can read a newspaper in any language knowing only a thousand words or so, which isn't many. Usually we express ourselves within that small vocabulary. We are not really skilled in the subtlety of words.

Speech, feelings, and body language shape how we relate to one another. One of the important aspects of communal living is not to select someone special to relate to, but to relate to everyone. If we pick out one or two persons whom we interact with and feel we can handle, but forget about the rest of the community, that's not sufficient for harmonious community living. A community includes everyone, and each member has the duty and privilege of learning to relate to all.

How do we relate successfully in a way that minimizes misunderstandings and makes it pleasing to be together? One of the qualities mentioned in the *Mettā Sutta (Loving-Kindness Discourse)* is being "easy to speak to." This means being ready to give up our own point of view and accept the other person's. We are willing to admit we have made a mistake or say that we are sorry, and really mean it. We don't snap back when someone speaks to us, we try to listen to what they say. Listening and hearing are not the same thing. We can hear when there is sound of any kind, but listening is an entirely different matter. Listening means really picking up on what is happening. Creating our own viewpoint is one of the worst errors we make when we believe we are listening, especially when we have a self-image of being a good listener. Listening means being empty of self-importance and reacting to what we hear with empathy. It is an art and a skill, just as much as speaking is. It requires really being with the other person. Just listening with total attention to what is being said, without making up our own story about it, without our mental chatter, is part of compassion. It is also loving-kindness. Unless there is loving-kindness in our speech, it's going to come out wrong.

In a discourse mentioned earlier, the *Exposition of Nonconflict*, the Buddha tells us not to exaggerate and not to underrate; both are forms of lying. If we had fifteen hundred people here for a function, for instance, and we claimed we had fifteen thousand to make ourselves seem more important, we would not be truthful. It seems absurd to exaggerate like this, but people say all sorts of absurdities. I may, for example, distort the truth by saying something like, "You never say good morning to me first." Well, maybe you don't say this often, but "never" probably isn't the truth. We have to think before we speak. When we speak impulsively, there is a chance of being right but an equal chance of being wrong. It's a fifty-fifty proposition, and we shouldn't take such chances. There's ample time to deliberate and ponder.

There are occasions when we need to tell someone what should be done or what should be left undone. "I can't sleep with the window open," for example, or "You shouldn't step on my toes, it hurts." There's nothing wrong with that, except we need to take our time and not say it impulsively. First we have to arouse equanimity within our own heart. When we are peaceful again, then we can remember all the good attributes of the person we wish to address, we can feel at ease about our relationship, and we can say what is on our minds. Loving-kindness must be awakened, and if it isn't shining through our words, we're not communicating. We will cause rejection or misunderstanding, or at least bewilderment. When we cause rejection, we heap insult on top of injury—two negatives instead of one.

There's a formula in the *Exposition of Nonconflict* that is extremely useful: "If you want to say anything that could be hurtful and is untrue, don't say it. If you want to say anything that is helpful and is untrue, don't say it. If you know or want to say anything that could be hurtful and is true, don't say it. And if you want to say something that could be helpful and is true, find the right time." Sometimes the right time might be ten minutes later, or it could be ten days, or ten months, later.

There are occasions when you know or suspect that a person is in a process of change. Then it may not be necessary to say anything at all. There's something wrong with each of us, it's impossible to talk about all of it—we would never stop. Some things do need to be said at times, but often it is not necessary because it will all change anyway. What is helpful and true doesn't have to be appreciative, but the words must be loving. The right time to speak is when we are completely calm and the other person is attentive, at ease, and ready to listen. If there's anger, it's the wrong time. This means watchful examination and deliberate speech. Unless we learn these skills, we will have many emotional accidents in our relationships. Life does not have to be lived at random; it can be lived deliberately, step by step, all day long. But we can't have a schedule for our speech; our speech has to find its own timetable and content. It is important to remember what constitutes wrong speech and how much time we sometimes waste on speech! If we were to keep track we would find that, except for sleeping and moments of concentration and mindfulness, speech is constant, perhaps for eighteen hours a day. Wouldn't it pay, then, to be skillfull when speaking?

Skillful communication is not as easily learned as it might seem. Reacting pleasantly is only one part of it. Even when we want to say something positive to another person, we need to examine our motives and intentions. Am I just trying to make that person or myself feel good? We need to know what is most skillful. If we want to make the other person feel good, that's fine. If we want to make ourselves feel good, we should desist and reexamine our motivations. If we don't practice deliberate speech, it will come out instinctively and impulsively, especially if we are feeling some stress. So let's not take speech for granted.

In the evening when we go to bed, instead of thinking about physical comfort or discomfort let us recapitulate how much positivity or negativity we have generated during the day. What did we accomplish with our speech? Have the five hindrances *(pañca nīvaraṇa)* been a prominent part of our day? Have sensual desire, ill will, sloth and torpor, restlessness and worry, and skeptical doubt arisen? What can we do to lessen their impact?

How can we have more love, compassion, joy with others, and equanimity? We could make a balance sheet each evening. If we have said anything during the day that we now regret, we've lacked deliberation and lost mindfulness. There's no blame attached, only recognition.

"Recognition, no condemnation, and change"—with this old, tried and true formula, we introspect and purify. In the evening, after a full day's activities, we will find that some of our speech has not been really useful and helpful. We can accept that with equanimity and resolve to do better the next day.

We must never forget to look at our motivations. A do-gooder doesn't do much good anywhere. The good has to happen first in our own hearts. Only then can goodness and purity come out of it. We can't give away what we don't have. If the heart is pure and full of love, it will radiate that, and speech becomes of secondary importance. It's not the vocabulary that counts but the feeling behind it. Unless we repeatedly examine our motivations for talking, there will always be accidents. These may prey on our minds, and our meditation will suffer. But who is the one that suffers? We ourselves reap the results of our wrong speech, no one else.

Speech is so important that the Buddha gave a discourse about it to his own son, who was seven at the time. The Buddha had returned victoriously from his search for enlightenment. It was the first time he actually met his little son Rahula, and he explained to him in detail the unfortunate results of lying. He emphasized that wrong speech was the forerunner of losing all spiritual achievements.

The Buddha mentioned speech so often because people have great difficulty with it. Their speech usually lacks warmth and intimacy, not because of what they say but because of what they feel. The Buddha's guidelines are to generate unconditional love in our hearts, a love that does not depend on other people's lovability. Only the arahant—the fully enlightened one— is totally lovable. Everybody else has some defilements. It's useless to consider other people's defilements; the only defilements that are of any interest to us are our own. They are exactly the same as everybody else's, only in different proportions.

Wrong speech is not necessarily abusive; it can be unkind, sarcastic, self-congratulatory, or self-inflating. These are all unwholesome ways of speaking. We eradicate them through purification and recurrent deliberation, checking ourselves again and again.

Right speech includes not lying, not backbiting, not speaking unkindly or abusively, not gossiping, not chattering idly, not setting one person against another. Unless we use speech skillfully, polishing it so that it has the desired impact without unpleasant repercussions, we haven't heard the Buddha's words properly. This aspect of his teaching has great importance for all of us.

10

Accepting Oneself

*S*trangely, most people have difficulty loving themselves. One would think it would be the easiest thing in the world, because we are constantly concerned with ourselves. We are always interested in how much we can get, how well we can perform, how comfortable we can be. The Buddha said in a discourse that "one is dearest to oneself." So why is it so difficult to actually love ourselves?

Loving ourselves certainly does not mean indulging ourselves. Most people do not really love themselves because they have quite a few undesirable traits. Everybody has innumerable reactions, likes, and dislikes that would better be discarded. We judge ourselves, and while we like our positive attitudes, we dislike the others and try to suppress them. We do not want to acknowledge them. Dealing with ourselves that way is detrimental to our search for truth.

Another unskillful act is blaming ourselves for our mistakes, which makes matters twice as bad. With that comes fear and very often aggression. If we want to deal with ourselves in a balanced way, it also doesn't help to pretend that the unpleasant part does not exist—the part consisting of our aggressive, irritable, sensual, conceited tendencies. Pretending takes us away from reality, and we split ourselves into two personalities. We have all come across people who are too sweet to be true, but only through pretense and suppression.

Blaming others does not work either, as it will undoubtedly result in transferring our reactions to other people. We blame others for their deficiencies, real or imagined, or do not see them as ordinary human beings. Everyone lives in an unreal, ego-deluded world, but the world of judgment and blame is particularly unreal, because it considers everything either perfectly wonderful or absolutely terrible.

The truth is that we have six roots within us: three of good and three of evil. The evil are greed, hate, and delusion, but we also have their opposites: generosity, loving-kindness, and wisdom. If we investigate without anxiety, we can easily accept these six roots in ourselves and everybody else. They underlie everyone's behavior. Then we can look at ourselves a little more realistically, without blaming ourselves for the unwholesome roots or patting ourselves on the back for the wholesome ones, but rather acknowledging their existence within us. We can also accept other people clear-sightedly and relate to them more easily.

A world of black or white, where we see only wholesome or unwholesome people, does not exist; the only completely pure person is an arahant. In everyone else purity is largely a matter of degree. Differences among us in the degree of good and evil are minor and really do not matter. Everybody has the same job to do, to cultivate the wholesome tendencies and uproot the unwholesome ones.

We may all seem to be very different, but that is an illusion. All of us have the same problems and the same faculties to deal with them. We differ only in the length of training that we have had. When we have trained our minds for a number of lifetimes, that will have brought about a little more clarity and discernment.

Clarity of thinking comes from the purification of our emotions, which is difficult to do. We can do it successfully only when we do not identify with emotional upheavals. When we consider our emotions clearly and straightforwardly as part of the work that we do on ourselves, the sting of identification is removed, and the charge of "I'm so wonderful" or "I'm so terrible" is defused. Everyone is a human being with potentials and obstructions. If we can love this human being, this "me," with all its faculties and tendencies, then we can love others realistically, usefully, and helpfully. But if we discriminate, loving only the nice aspects and disliking the rest, we will never come to grips with reality. One day we will have to see things as they are. We are our own "working ground" *(kammaṭṭhāna)*.

If we look at ourselves in this manner, we will learn to love ourselves in a wholesome way—just as, the Buddha says, "a mother at the risk of her own life loves and protects her child." If we want a realistic relationship with ourselves that is conducive to growth, then we need to become our own mother. A sensible mother can distinguish between behavior that is useful for her child and that which is detrimental, but she does not stop loving the child when it misbehaves. This may be one of the most important aspects to consider in ourselves. Everyone, at one time or another, misbehaves in thought, speech, or action—most frequently in thought, fairly frequently in speech, and not so often in action. What do we do with that? What would a mother do? She would tell the child not to do it again, reassure the child of her continual love, and get on with the job of bringing up her child. Maybe we can start bringing up ourselves.

The whole of this training is a matter of maturing. Maturity brings wisdom, which is unfortunately not connected to age. If it were, it would be easier, and we would have a sort of guarantee of success. But in reality it is hard work, a job to be done by each one of us. First we learn recognition, then we make sure we are not condemning ourselves, but rather accepting that "This is the way it is." The third step is change. Recognition may be the hardest part for most people—it is not easy to see what goes on inside us. This is the most important and most interesting aspect of contemplation.

We lead a contemplative life, but that does not mean we sit in meditation all day long. A contemplative life means that we consider every aspect of what happens as part of a learning experience. We remain introspective in all circumstances. When we are outgoing—when we adopt what the Buddha termed "exuberance of youth" and engage in the world with our thoughts, speech, and action—we need to recollect ourselves and return within. A contemplative life in some religious orders means a life of prayer. In our way, it is a combination of meditation and lifestyle. The contemplative life continues all the time. Outwardly one can do exactly the same thing with or without inner recollection. Contemplation is the most important ingredient of introspection. It is not necessary to sit still all day and watch our breath. Every move, every thought, every word can give rise to understanding.

This kind of work will bring about a deep inner security that is rooted in reality. Most people wish and hope for this kind of assurance but are unable to express their longing, let alone realize it. Living in a myth, living in constant hope or fear denies inner strength. The feeling of security arises when we see reality inside ourselves, and see the same reality in everyone else, and come to terms with it.

Let us accept that the Buddha knew the truth when he said everybody has seven underlying tendencies: sensual desire, ill will, speculative views, skeptical doubt, conceit, craving for continued existence, and ignorance. We can find them in ourselves, smile at them and say, Well, there you are. I'll do something about you.

The contemplative life is often lived with a heavy heart. Lacking joy, we may compensate by being outgoing. This does not work. One should cultivate lightheartedness but stay within. There is nothing to be worried or fearful about, nothing that is too difficult. Dhamma means the law of nature, and we are manifesting this law all the time. We cannot escape the law of nature. Wherever we are, we are the Dhamma, we are impermanent (anicca), unfulfilled (dukkha), and have no core substance (anattā). It does not matter whether we sit here or on the moon, it is the same everywhere. We need a lighthearted approach to our difficulties and those of everyone else. No exuberance and outpouring, but rather a constant inwardness that contains a bit of amusement. That works best. If we have a sense of humor about ourselves, it is much easier to love ourselves properly. It is also much easier to love everybody else.

There used to be a television show in America called "People Are Funny." We do have the oddest reactions. When they are analyzed and taken apart, they are often found to be absurd. We have very strange desires and wishes and unrealistic images of ourselves. People *are* funny—it is quite true—so why not see that side of ourselves? It makes it easier to accept what we find so unacceptable in ourselves and others.

There is one aspect of human life that we cannot change: life keeps on happening moment after moment. We have all been meditating here for some time. What does the world care? It just keeps on going. The only ones who care, who get perturbed, are our own hearts and minds. When there is perturbation, upheaval, unreality, and absurdity, then there is also unhappiness. This is quite unnecessary. Everything just is. If we learn to approach all happenings with more equanimity, the work of purification is much easier. This is our work, our own purification, and it can only be done by each of us individually.

If we remember what we are doing, keep at it day after day without forgetting, and continue to meditate without expecting great results, little by little purification does happen. That, too, just is. As we keep chipping away at the defilements, we realize more and more there is no happiness to be found in them. Few people want to hang on to unhappiness. Eventually one runs out of things to do outside of the work on oneself. As this happens again and again, a change takes place. It may be slow, but when we have been here so many lifetimes, what is a day, a month, a year, ten years?

There is nothing else to do, and there is nowhere else to go. The earth is moving in a circle, life is moving from birth to death. It is all happening without our help. The only thing we need to do is to see and understand reality. When we do, we find that love for ourselves and others arises naturally, because that is the heart's real work—to love. If we have also seen the unloving side of ourselves and have done the work of purification, then it is no longer an effort or a deliberate attempt that we make, but a natural function of our inner feelings, directed inward but shining outward.

The inward direction is an important aspect of our contemplative life. Whatever happens inside has direct repercussions on what takes place outside. The inner light and purity cannot be hidden, nor can the defilements.

We sometimes think we can portray ourselves as something we are not. That is not possible. The Buddha said that one only knows a person after having heard him speak many times and having lived with him for a long time. People generally try to show themselves off as something better than they really are. Then, of course, they become disappointed with themselves when they fail, and equally disappointed in others. Knowing ourselves in a caring and realistic way opens our heart and brings buoyancy to our introspection. By accepting ourselves and others as we truly are, our job of purification, chipping away at the defilements, becomes much easier.

11

Ideal Solitude

ॐ **I**n the *Sutta Nipāta* we find a discourse called *The Rhinoceros Horn,* in which the Buddha compares the solitary sage with the single horn of the rhinoceros. The Buddha praises the solitary life, and the refrain to every stanza of the sutta is "Wander alone, a rhinoceros horn."

There are two kinds of solitude, that of the mind *(citta-viveka)* and that of the body *(kāya-viveka)*. Everyone is familiar with solitude of the body. We go away and sit by ourselves in a room or cave, or we tell the people we are living with that we want to be left alone. We usually like such solitude for short periods. If we remain alone longer, it is often because we are unable to get along with others or fear them because we do not have enough love in our heart. Often we may experience loneliness.

When we live in a family or community, it is sometimes difficult to find physical solitude. Everybody should have some time each day to be on their own, so that they can really feel alone. But this is not the only kind of aloneness. Mental solitude is an important factor for practice. Unless we are able to arouse it, we will not be able to discover through introspection how we must change.

Mental solitude means first and foremost not depending on others for approval, for companionship, for relationships. It does not mean that we become unfriendly toward others, just that we are mentally independent. The solitary mind is a strong mind, because it knows how to stand still. It is able to be alone and introspect and also be loving toward others. If another person is kind to us, well and good. If that is not the case, that is fine too. Solitude in the mind means also that we can be alone in the midst of a crowd. Even if the crowd is boisterous, we can still operate from our own center, giving out love without being influenced by what is happening around us.

The horn of a rhinoceros is straight and solid and so strong that we cannot bend it. Can our minds be like that? Mental solitude cuts out idle chatter. Talking about nothing at all, just letting off steam, is detrimental to spiritual growth. When we let the steam escape from a pot, we cannot cook our food. Our practice can be likened to keeping the heat on. If we turn off the heat again and again, that inner process is stopped. It is much better to let the steam accumulate and find out what is cooking. That is the most important work we can do.

Sometimes we think, People are talking about me! That does not matter—we are the owners of our own karma. If somebody talks about us, it is their karma. If we get upset, that is our karma. Taking interest in what is being said about us shows that we are dependent on people's approval. But who is approving of whom? Maybe the five khandhas—body, feeling, perception, mental formations, and consciousness—are approving? Or possibly the hair of the head, the hair of the body, nails, teeth, and skin? Which "self" is approving, the good one, the bad one, the mediocre one, or maybe the nonself?

Unless we can find a feeling of solidity in our own center, a place where there is no movement, we are always going to feel insecure. Nobody, not even the Buddha, can be liked by everyone. Because we have defilements, we are always on the lookout for everybody else's pollutions. None of that matters. The only thing of significance is mindfulness, being totally attentive to what we are doing, feeling, thinking. It is so easy to forget this. There is always somebody to talk with or another cup of tea to drink. That is how the world lives and its inhabitants are mostly unhappy. But the Buddha's path leads out of the world to independent happiness.

Ideal mental solitude means we have removed ourselves from the future and the past, and we stand straight and alone. If we are attached to the future, there is worry, and if we hanker after the past, there will be either desire or rejection.

Solitude can be fully experienced only when there is inner peace. Otherwise loneliness pushes us to remedy feelings of emptiness and loss. "Where is everybody? What can I do without some companionship? I must discuss my problems." Mindfulness is able to take care of all that, because it arises in the present moment and has nothing to do with the future or past. It keeps us totally occupied and saves us from making mistakes. The greater our mindfulness, the fewer the mistakes. Errors on the mundane level have repercussions for the spiritual path. When our lack of mindfulness leads us to inflict dukkha on ourselves, we will try again and again to find someone who is to blame or someone who can distract us.

Ideal solitude arises when a person can be alone or with others and retain the same inner calm, not getting caught in someone else's difficulties. We may respond in an appropriate manner, but we are not affected. We all have our own inner life, but we get to know it well only when the mind stops chattering and we can attend to our inner feelings. Once we have seen what is happening inside of us, we will want to change some of it. Only the fully enlightened one—an arahant—has an inner life that needs no improvement. Our inner stress and lack of peace push us to find someone who will remove our dukkha, but only we can do it.

The solitary mind can have profound and original thoughts, whereas a dependent mind thinks in clichés because it wants approval. A worldly mind that understands only superficialities cannot grasp the profundity of the Buddha's teaching.

The main value of a solitary mind is imperturbability. It cannot be shaken and will stand without support, like a big tree. If the mind does not have enough vigor to stand on it's own, it will not have the strength and determination to fulfill the Dhamma. A side benefit is better memory. A mind at ease, which stands on its own and is not filled with the desire to remove dukkha, can remember a lot.

Our practice includes being on our own some time each day to introspect and contemplate. Reading, talking, and listening are all forms of communication that are necessary at times. But it is essential to have time for self-inquiry: What is happening within me? What am I feeling? Is it wholesome or not? Am I perfectly contented on my own? How much self-concern is there? Is the Dhamma my guide, or am I bewildered?

Health, wealth, and youth do not spare us from dukkha. But they may cover it up. Ill health, poverty, and old age make it easier to realize the unsatisfactoriness of our existence. When we are alone, that is the time to get to know ourselves. We can investigate the meaning of the Dhamma we have heard, and strive to actualize those aspects most meaningful for us.

A Dhamma community is an ideal place to practice this. At times, in communal living, there is togetherness and lovingness and service. These should be the results of loving-kindness, not of trying to get away from dukkha. Next time we start a conversation, let us first investigate: Why am I having this discussion? Is it necessary, or am I bored and want to get away from my problems?

Clear comprehension is the mental factor that joins with mindfulness to give purpose and direction. We examine whether our speech and actions have the right purpose, whether we are using skillful means, and whether we have accomplished our initial purpose. If we have no clear-cut direction, idle chatter results. Even in meditation the mind chatters idly, which is due to lack of training. When we practice clear comprehension, we stop for a moment and examine the whole situation before plunging in. This may become one of our skillful habits, not often found in the world.

An important aspect of the Buddha's teaching is the combination of clear comprehension with mindfulness. The Buddha often recommends this pair as the way out of all sorrow, and we need to practice it in small, daily efforts: learning something new, recalling a Dhamma sentence, memorizing a line of chanting, gaining a new insight into ourselves, realizing some aspect of reality. Such a mind gains strength and self-confidence.

Renunciation is the greatest help in gaining self-confidence. One knows one can get along without practically everything, even food, for quite some time. Once the Buddha went to a village where nobody had any faith in him. Nobody in the village paid any attention to him, and he received no alms food at all. He went to the outskirts and sat down on a bit of straw and meditated. Another ascetic, who saw that the Buddha had not received any food, commiserated with him: "You must be feeling very bad, not having anything to eat. I'm very sorry. You don't even have a nice place to sleep, just straw." The Buddha replied: "Feeders on joy we are. Inner joy can feed us for many days."

One can get along without many things when we give them up voluntarily. If someone tries to take our belongings, we resist, which is dukkha. But when we practice self-denial, the mind gains strength and learns to stand on its own. Self-confidence gives it a really strong backbone.

The Buddha did not advocate extreme ascetic practices. But we could give up some activities—for instance, afternoon conversations—and contemplate instead. Afterward the mind feels contented with its efforts. The more effort one makes, the more satisfaction arises.

12

Be Nobody

eing happy also means being peaceful, but quite often people do not really want to direct their attention to that. Peacefulness connotes "not interesting" or "not enough happening," the absence of proliferations *(papañca)* or excitement. Yet peace is very hard to find anywhere. It is difficult to attain, and very few people really work at it. Peace seems to negate life, to deny our personal supremacy. Only those who practice a spiritual discipline care to direct their mind toward it.

Our natural tendency is to cultivate our superiority, which often falls into the other extreme of inferiority. So long as we have our own superiority in mind, we cannot find peace. All we find is a power game: "Anything you can do, I can do better." Or at times when it is quite obvious that this is not so, then it's "Anything you can do, I cannot do as well." There are moments of truth in everyone's life when one sees quite clearly that one can't do everything as well as the next person, whether it's sweeping a path or writing a book.

A feeling of superiority or inferiority is the opposite of peacefulness. A display of one's abilities, or the lack of them, will produce restlessness. There is always the reaching out, the craving for a result in the form of other people's admiration or their denial of it. When they deny it, there is warfare. When they affirm it, there is victory.

In war there is never a winner, only losers. No matter who signs the peace treaty first, both sides lose. The same applies to a feeling of being victorious, of being the one who knows better or who is stronger or cleverer. Battle and peace do not go well together.

One wonders in the end, Does anybody really want peace? Is anybody really trying to get it? We must inquire into our innermost hearts if peace is what we really want. Such an inquiry is difficult. Most people have a thick steel door in front of their hearts. They cannot find out what is going on inside. But everyone needs to try to get in as far as possible and check their priorities.

In moments of turmoil, when we are either not getting the supremacy we want or we feel really inferior, then all we desire is peace. When our unrest and feeling of inferiority subside, then what happens? Is it really peace we want? Or do we want to be somebody special, somebody important or lovable?

A "somebody" never has peace. There is an interesting simile about a mango tree. A king went riding in the forest and encountered a mango tree laden with fruit. He said to his servants, "Go back in the evening and collect the mangoes," because he wanted them for the royal dining table. The servants went back to the forest but returned to the palace empty-handed. "Sorry, your majesty," they told the king, "the mangoes were all gone, there was not a single mango left on the tree." The king thought the servants had been too lazy to go back to the forest, so he rode out to see for himself. What he saw instead of a beautiful mango tree laden with fruit was a pitiful, bedraggled tree. Someone had broken all the branches to take the fruit. As the king rode a little farther, he came upon another mango tree, beautiful in all its green splendor, but without a single fruit. Nobody had wanted to go near it. It bore no fruit, so it was left in peace. The king went back to his palace, gave his royal crown and scepter to his ministers, and said, "You may now have the kingdom, I am going to live in a hut in the forest."

When one is nobody and has nothing, there is no danger of warfare or attack, and there is peace. The mango tree laden with fruit did not have a moment's peace; everybody wanted its fruit. If we really want peace, we have to be nobody. Neither important, nor clever, nor beautiful, nor famous, nor right, nor in charge of anything. We need to be unobtrusive and have as few attributes as possible. The mango tree with no fruit was standing peacefully in all its splendor, giving shade. To be nobody does not mean doing nothing. It means acting without self-display and without craving for results. The mango tree had shade to give, but it did not display its wares or fret whether anyone wanted its shade. This ability allows for inner peace. It is a rare ability, because most people vacillate from one extreme to another, either doing nothing and thinking, "Let them see how they get along without me," or being in charge and projecting their views and ideas.

Being somebody, it seems, is so much more ingrained and important than having peace. So we need to inquire with great care what we are truly looking for. What is it that we want out of life? If we want to be important, appreciated, and loved, then we have to take their opposites in stride. Every positive brings with it a negative, just as the sun throws shadows. If we want one, we must accept the other, without moaning about it.

But if we really want a peaceful heart and mind, inner security, and stability, then we have to give up wanting to be somebody, anybody. Body and mind will not disappear because of that; what subsides is the urge to affirm the importance and supremacy of this particular person whom I call "me."

Every human being considers himself or herself important. There are billions of people on this globe, how many will mourn us? Count them for a moment. Six or eight, or twelve or fifteen, out of all these billions. Maybe we have a vastly exaggerated idea of our own importance. The more we understand this, the easier life is.

Wanting to be somebody is dangerous. It is like playing with a fire, and it hurts constantly. And other people will not play by our rules. People who really manage to be somebody, like heads of state, invariably need a bodyguard because they are in danger of their lives.

Among the countless things in our world—all the people, animals, and natural and man-made objects—the only ones we have any jurisdiction over are our own heart and mind. If we really want to be somebody, we could try to be that rare person who is in charge of his own heart and mind. Becoming somebody like that is not only very rare, it also brings the most beneficial results. Such a person does not fall into the trap of the defilements.

There is a story about Achaan Cha, a famous meditation master in Northeast Thailand. He was once accused of having a lot of hatred. Achaan Cha replied, "That may be so, but I don't make any use of it." An answer like this comes from a deep understanding of one's own nature. It is a rare person who will not allow himself defiled thought, speech, or action. Such a person is really somebody. He does not have to prove it to anyone else because it is quite obvious, not to mention that he has no desire to prove anything. There is only one abiding interest and that is one's own peace of mind.

When we have peace of mind as our priority, everything in the mind and all speech or action is directed toward it. Anything that does not create peace of mind is discarded. We must not confuse this with being right or having the last word, however. Others need not agree. Peace of mind is our own. We can all find it if we make the effort.

13

War and Peace

*W*ar and peace—the epic saga of humanity—are all that our history books contain because they are what our hearts contain.

If you have ever read Don Quixote, you will remember that he was fighting windmills. Don Quixote believed himself to be a great warrior. He thought that every windmill he came across was an enemy and battled with it. That is exactly what we do within our hearts and that is why this story has such an everlasting appeal. It tells us about ourselves. Writers and poets have always sought to tell us who we are. Mostly we do not listen, because it does not help when somebody else tells us what is wrong with us. We have to find out for ourselves, and most people do not want to do that.

What does it really mean to fight windmills? It means fighting nothing important or real, just imaginary enemies and battles—trifling matters that we build into something solid and formidable. We say, "I can't stand that," and we start fighting; "I don't like him," and a battle ensues; "I feel so unhappy," and an inner war rages. We hardly ever know what we are so unhappy about. The weather? Food? People? Work? Leisure? The country? Anything at all will usually do. Why does this happen to us? Because of our resistance to letting go and becoming what we really are, namely, nothing. Nobody cares to be that.

Everybody wants to be somebody, somebody who knows and acts, who has certain attributes, views, opinions, and ideas, even if it is only Don Quixote tilting against windmills. We even hold on to patently wrong views because they make the "I" more solid. We may think it is negative and depressing to be nobody and have nothing. But in fact, as we may find out for ourselves, it is the most exhilarating and liberating feeling we can ever have. But because we fear that windmills might attack us, we do not let go of our illusions.

Why can we not have peace in the world? Because nobody wants to disarm. Not a single country is ready to sign a total disarmament pact. All of us bemoan this fact, but have we ever looked to see whether *we* have disarmed? When we have not done so, is it any wonder that nobody else has? Nobody wants to be the first one without weapons, out of fear that others might attack. Does it really matter? If there is nobody there, who can be conquered? How can there be a victory over nobody? Let those who fight win every war, all that matters is to have peace in one's heart.

War manifests itself externally in violence, aggression, and killing. But how does it reveal itself internally? We each carry an arsenal within us: our ill will and anger, our desires and cravings. But we ourselves are hurt by the violence we carry within us. The proof is that we do not feel peaceful inside. Sometimes another person comes within range and is wounded; sometimes a bomb goes off in our heart and causes a disaster.

We need not believe anything, we can just find out whether there is peace and joy in our hearts. If they are lacking, most people try to find them outside of themselves. That is how all wars start. It is always the other country's fault, and if one cannot find anyone to blame, then it becomes a case of needing more *Lebensraum,* more room for expansion, more territorial sovereignty. In personal terms, one needs more entertainment, more pleasure, more comfort, more distractions. If we cannot find anyone else to blame for our lack of peace, then we believe it to be an unfulfilled need.

Few of us come to see that the windmills we tilt against are imaginary, that they will vanish if we do not endow them with strength and importance, that we can open our hearts without fear and gently, gradually let go of our preconceived notions and opinions, our views and ideas, our habits and reactions. When all that fades away, what do we have left? A large, open space that we can fill with whatever we like. If we are wise, we will fill it with love, compassion, and equanimity. Then there is nothing left to fight. Only joy and peacefulness remain. We cannot find these outside of ourselves. There is no opening in us through which peace might enter. We have to start within and work outward. Until we are clear about this, we will always find another crusade.

Imagine what it was like in the days of the crusades! There were those noble knights who spent all their wealth on equipping themselves with the most modern and advanced weapons, outfitting horses and troops, and then setting off to bring religion to the infidels. Some died on the way because of hardships and battles, and those who reached their destination, the Holy Land, still did not get any results, only more warfare. When we look at this today, it seems utterly foolish, even ridiculous.

Yet we do the same in our own lives. If, for instance, we open our diary and read about something that upset us three or four years ago, it may now seem quite absurd. We cannot remember why it was so important. We are constantly engaged in such foolishness over trifles, and we expend much energy trying to work them out to our satisfaction. Would it not be much better to forget such mental formations and attend to what is really important? There is only one thing that is important to every being, and that is a peaceful and happy heart. This cannot be bought or found, nor can it be given away. Ramana Maharshi, a sage in southern India, said: "Peace and happiness are not our birthright. Whoever has attained them has done so by continual effort."

Some people have an idea that peace and happiness are synonymous with doing nothing, having no duties or responsibilities, and being looked after by others. That is laziness. To gain peace and happiness we have to make unrelenting effort in our own hearts. We cannot achieve it by trying to acquire more and more, only by wanting less, by becoming emptier and emptier until there is just open space to be filled with peace and happiness. As long as our hearts are full of likes and dislikes, how can peace and happiness find room?

We can find peace within ourselves in any situation, place, or circumstance, but only through effort, not through distraction. The world offers distractions and sense contacts, and they are often quite tempting. The more action there is, the more distracted the mind can be and the less we have to look at our own dukkha. When we take the time and opportunity to introspect, we find a different inner reality from the one we imagined. Many people quickly look away again—they do not want to know about it. It is nobody's fault that there is dukkha. The only cure is letting go. It is really quite simple, but few people believe this enough to try it out.

There is a well-known simile about a monkey trap of the kind used in Asia—a wooden container with a small opening. Inside lies a sweet. The monkey, attracted by the sweet, puts his paw into the opening and grasps the sweet. When he wants to draw his paw out again, he cannot get his fist with the sweet through the narrow opening. He is trapped until the hunter comes and captures him. He does not realize that all he has to do to be free is to let go of the sweet.

That is what our lives are all about. It traps us because we want it nice and sweet. Not being able to let go, we are caught in the ever recurring cycle of happiness and unhappiness, hope and despair. We never try to free ourselves by letting go; indeed, we resist and reject such a notion. Yet we all agree that all that matters are peace and happiness, which can only exist in a free mind and heart.

There is a lovely story from Nazrudin, a Sufi master, who was gifted in telling absurd tales. One day, the story goes, he sent one of his disciples to the market and asked him to buy him a bag of chilies. The disciple did as requested and brought the bag to Nazrudin, who began to eat the chilies, one after another. Soon his face turned red, his nose started running, his eyes began to water, and he was choking. The disciple observed this for a while with awe and then said: "Sir, your face is turning red, your eyes are watering, and you are choking. Why don't you stop eating these chilies?" Nazrudin replied: "I am waiting for a sweet one."

The teaching aid of chilies! We, too, are waiting for something, somewhere, that will create peace and happiness for us. Meanwhile there is nothing but dukkha. Our eyes are watering, our noses are running, but we still don't set aside our creations. There must be a sweet one at the bottom of the bag! It is no use thinking, hearing, or reading about it: we must look inside our own hearts and grasp the reality within. The more the heart is wanting and desiring, the harder and more difficult life becomes.

Why fight all these windmills? We have built them, so we can dismantle them too. It is rewarding to see what clutters our hearts and minds. When we do so, we find emotion after emotion. Instead of justifying them or making allowances, we realize that they constitute the world's battlegrounds. So we start dismantling our weapons, and disarmament becomes a reality.

Nuts and Bolts

14
Many Drops Fill a Bucket

კ **R**ight effort, another step on the Noble Eightfold Path, is essential to both worldly endeavors and spiritual practice. Yet very often we misunderstand it and make mistakes. Most often we err on the side of too little effort.

Right effort happens when we involve all our physical and mental capacities. We all have slight differences in our abilities, so it is up to each of us to know what our best effort is. In the evening when we go to bed, we can recapitulate the happenings of the day and can ask ourselves, Have I really tried today? Have I extended myself to my personal limit, or did I take it as easy as I could? Did I try to increase my self-discipline a little more than yesterday? Did I try to get up five minutes earlier? Did I try to remember two more lines of the teaching? Did I try to sit longer in one position or concentrate a little longer? Did I have fewer negative thoughts today? We don't need to ask anyone else whether our effort was right or not. We must determine this ourselves.

Many drops of water fill a bucket, and life is made up of small incidents. Great events might come once or twice in a lifetime, but every day small events happen from morning to night. Our effort is just like the drops of water filling the bucket: very small but just a little more than yesterday. Eventually, the bucket will be filled. One day we make one last effort that totally removes the delusion of self. But unless we put in effort every day, be it ever so small, this will never happen.

We are interested in pleasant feelings and want to be comfortable. Often more effort feels uncomfortable. But whether we are comfortable or not does not really matter. Our concern about comfort won't make anything important happen. On the contrary, it undermines effort. If we don't disregard personal comfort occasionally, we will eventually find ourselves without incentive, without motivation. If we never extend our limits at all, in the end we will lose sight of our goal and will only seek comfort. Sliding downhill is much easier than climbing up. The law of gravity that prevails over the body prevails equally over the mind.

Making an extra effort gives us a great deal of satisfaction. We can recollect how we have spent our day with a contented mind, or whether we have tried to make some extra effort and succeeded. We should never let a day go by without recollection. Otherwise, how can we learn what is important and what isn't?

Only one single moment exists, and that's the present one. The future is a figment of the imagination. When the future really happens, it becomes the present. The future never turns out the way we imagined because the person who imagined it and the person who experiences it aren't the same. Projecting into the future and delving into the past are both a waste of time. The past is irrevocably gone. If we have done anything wrong in the past, we should learn from it so as not to repeat it—that's the only worthwhile remembrance to pursue. The past is quickly dealt with and just as profitably dropped.

This particular moment is the only one we can experience. When we have a whole day before us, it's like a whole lifetime. In the morning we are newly born, fresh and bright, and during that day we live a whole life with all kinds of emotions—like, dislike, worry, disturbance, fear, anxiety, acceptance, tolerance, patience, love, compassion. They all happen in one and the same day, and if we don't make an effort also in that same day, we've wasted precious time. If this becomes habitual, we're liable to waste a good human life.

According to the Buddha's words, the human realm is the best possible realm in which to attain enlightenment. There is dukkha here to spur us on, and enough *sukha* (pleasure) to keep a balance. However, sukha can also be misleading because most people mistakenly believe that, if they fix things right, they might jump from pleasure to pleasure without having to experience dukkha. It's a misconception. Nonetheless, this is the best realm for spiritual attainment, for each of us has a mind that can free itself of all fetters. But without effort this will never happen.

Sometimes people make an effort that demands very much of them but is really the wrong kind of effort, for it is totally obsessed with results. Obsession with results produces tension, which generates headaches, back-aches, worries, and restlessness. Expectations lead to disappointments. When we have only the result in mind, obviously we can't pay attention to the task at hand. But if we let go of whatever we're trying to achieve and apply our whole mindfulness and attention to the effort we're making, we have a chance to succeed without creating tension.

Sometimes people get a headache from meditation and conclude that there must be something wrong with the meditation. It doesn't occur to them that there could be something wrong with their effort. They're so obsessed with achieving concentration that they create discomfort and make no meditative progress.

Effort has its own reward: the satisfaction of having made the effort, and also added mental strength. When we train the body, as we know, we strengthen our muscles, increase our resistance to fatigue, and gain the abil-ity to handle difficult tasks more easily. The same is true about the mind. By making a little more effort than before, we stretch the mind, and if we continue, the mind stays expanded. But if we let up, we contract to where we were, like a rubber band. Eventually we can stretch the mind so that it cannot snap back anymore. It becomes pliable, malleable, encompassing, and begins to see the whole gamut of universal experiences rather than the little speck of personal space that each of us occupies.

Effort has to be constant and should not alternate between nothing one day and too much the next. Lack of constancy can easily result in our feel-ing sorry for ourselves and becoming tired and discontented. Steady effort—day after day, minute after minute, and checking at the end of the day whether we have tried to do just a little more than yesterday—this brings a feeling of satisfaction. If we learn one or two words at a time, even-tually we know the whole recitation. One minute of concentration per day results in an hour of concentration in two months.

A big obstacle is our desire for pleasant feelings, mostly physical ones. Sometimes such feelings arise, sometimes not. Basically there are only three kinds of feeling: pleasant, unpleasant, and neutral. (The neutral ones tend toward pleasantness, since they do not create any suffering for us.) Our instinctive reactions direct us to cling to pleasant feelings and avoid unpleasant ones. But since pleasure can never be sustained, our quest for it keeps us occupied until the end of life and is the linking cause of our rebirth. It is a totally futile preoccupation, and the sooner we realize what we are doing and learn to let go, the sooner we can rightly say we are practicing Dhamma.

When we gain strength through sustained effort, we experience the inner joy of knowing that we have invested our wholehearted effort in the practice of becoming enlightened. Nothing compares to this in the world. Everything else we do is geared toward survival, which is, of course, necessary but not fulfilling.

Whatever we do, whether we write a book or chop carrots, it only matters how we do it. Most people believe writing a book is much more important than chopping vegetables. But whenever we act with total mindfulness and let go of our desire for results—which is easier when chopping carrots than when writing a book—we are observing the Buddha's guidelines. It's not *I* who am doing it, it's just something that needs to be done. That's a useful criterion for any activity. The "I" that enters the scene is the old troublemaker, creating all sorts of waves of emotions, which do not bring a happy and tranquil mind.

When we watch our reactions, we realize that they are preprogrammed. We're programmed by instinct and craving, and also by our firmly anchored belief in our identity. Most people imagine they're in control of their lives, because they're thinking and their mind is working. In reality we are just reacting. If we were truly in control, as an arahant would be, then we would surely never be unhappy, worried, fearful, or upset. It would be utter foolishness to react in such ways voluntarily.

When we become more aware, we realize that our reactions are self-generated and self-perpetuating, without rhyme or reason. We will be amazed and determined to put an end to them.

This awareness requires daily, minute-by-minute effort, just a fraction more than yesterday. Eventually the whole day is pleasant effort, which doesn't deteriorate into compulsory censure. Once the motivation has started, it's like getting a stuck car rolling again. Getting it unstuck is difficult, but once the wheels are turning, the momentum keeps them going. Motivation has to come from within ourselves, and if we have insight, we formulate it as "I really want to get out of dukkha," never as "I would prefer to have it pleasant." The latter is a lost cause, since we can't always have pleasant feelings, and the wish for comfort and ease deprives us of strong resolution. To get out of dukkha requires recognition and change. These bring the satisfaction of knowing that we are working toward the highest ideals.

If we think, speak, and act with mindfulness, paying undivided attention to mind and body, we support our meditation practice and begin to penetrate our self-delusion. We become aware of the action without an actor. It's always the action that counts—the purity of our motivation—and not the result.

When we ask ourselves, "Why am I experiencing dukkha? What is displeasing me?" without getting caught in reactions, every day is a joy to live. If not, something is wrong in our thinking. Each day is meant for renewed effort to overcome selfhood. Hot or cold, wet or dry, good food or bad—it makes no difference. All efforts go in one direction: to penetrate the illusion of an owner of mind and body.

Each of us must judge right effort for ourselves. We can't say to someone, "You're not making enough effort" or "You're making too much." We all have different capacities and tendencies, difficulties and karmic results, but we should discover our maximum potential. The world usually runs on minimal effort.

Our physical and mental aspects are closely bound up with each other. In order to meditate, for instance, we sit down, which is a physical action that supports our mental efforts. Mindfulness keeps the mental and physical together. Within this framework of mind and body, we are deluded into believing that these two are "me." When we become aware how often the "I" gets in the way of our happiness, we will very likely become disenchanted with it and see that it is really not worth having around. This "I" is constantly creating thoughts and emotions, which disturb our inner peacefulness.

Disenchantment with the "I" is the first step toward letting go of our identifications and is bound up with effort. Even the effort itself is already a step in that direction. Whenever we give ourselves wholeheartedly to any wholesome action, the "I" shrinks.

In the evening, as I said, we can check up on how our day has gone. Have I tried a little harder, or have I wasted my precious time? Have I remembered more of the teaching? There's no blame attached, no condemnation, if the answer is negative. The next morning, a new life starts and a new resolution is appropriate.

That way each day becomes buoyant. We never get the "I wish the day were over" feeling. We spend every moment profitably and joyfully.

Joy is an active ingredient in the holy life, comparable to yeast in bread. Without joy the holy life cannot rise to its full height. So enjoy every moment and especially each effort.

15
Nonduality

◂ ruth occupies an important position in the Buddha's teaching. The Four Noble Truths are the hub of the wheel of the Dhamma, and truth *(sacca)* is one of the ten perfections to be cultivated for purification. If we want to find an end to suffering, we have to find truth at its deepest level. The moral precepts, including "not lying," are basic tools by which we practice letting go, which we must do if we want to find this basic underlying truth of all existence. This includes letting go of our weakest and our strongest attachments, many of which we do not even recognize.

To get to the bottom of truth, we have to get to the bottom of ourselves, and that is not easy because we do not love ourselves. The reason we do not love ourselves and the reason we want to learn to love ourselves better is because we feel self-hatred, and we are caught in the world of duality.

So long as we float around in the world of duality, we cannot get to the bottom of truth. In the *Sutta Nipāta* we find the interesting admonition that, in order to prevent attachments, one should not have associates. The idea is that this results in neither love nor hate, so that only equanimity—even-mindedness toward all that exists—remains. With equanimity we are no longer suspended between the dualities of good and bad, love and hate, friend and enemy, but are able to let go, to get to the bottom, where truth can be found.

Think of a vast ocean. If we cling to things, we cannot reach any depth. Our attachments—people, ideas, and views that we consider ours and believe to be right and useful—keep us from getting in touch with absolute truth. Our reactions, our likes and dislikes, hold us in suspense. While it is more pleasant to like something or someone, both like and dislike are due to attachments. So too are the distractions we face in meditation. Just as we are attached to the food we eat, so we are attached to food for the mind. Our thoughts go here and there, picking up tidbits. We move from thought to breath and back again, suspended in the world of duality and never touching rock bottom.

Depth of understanding makes release from suffering possible. When we go deeper and deeper and find no core, we learn to let go of even deep-seated attachments. Whether what we find within us is pure and commendable or impure and unpleasant makes no difference. All mental states that we own and cherish keep us in duality, in midair, in insecurity, and cannot bring an end to suffering. One moment all might be well in our world and we love everyone, but five minutes later we might react with hate and rejection.

Even if we agree with the Buddha's words and find them plausible, without the certainty of personal experience they will be of limited assistance. To have direct knowledge, we must sink like a stone, untied to anything, down to the bottom of all our obstructions. To see the truth, we need a powerful mind, a weighty mind. As long as the mind is interested in petty concerns, it will not have sufficient weight to attain deep understanding.

Most of our minds are in the bantamweight class. The punch of a heavyweight really carries a lot of force, a bantamweight's much less. Our lightweight minds are attached everywhere, to people and their opinions, to the duality of pure and impure, right and wrong.

Why do we take everything so personally instead of seeing universal truths? That seems to be the biggest difference between living at ease and living at loggerheads with ourselves and others. Hate and greed are not personal manifestations, nobody has a singular claim on them, they belong to humanity. If we learned to let go of taking our mind states personally, we would be rid of a serious impediment. Greed and hate exist. By the same token non-greed and non-hate also exist. Do we own the whole lot at once? Or do we own them in succession, five minutes at a time? Why own any of them? They just exist. When we see that, we sink into the depths of the Buddha's vision.

The deepest truth of the Buddha's teaching shows us that there is no individual person. We may accept this intellectually and experience it at an emotional level, but as long as we have not let go of owning body and mind, we will continue to think of ourselves as special. This is a gradual process.

In meditation we learn to let go of ideas and stories and attend to the meditation subject. If we do not let go, we cannot sink into the meditation. The mind has to be a heavyweight for that too. The ordinary mind bobs around on the waves of thoughts and feelings, even in meditation. If we do not practice throughout the day, our meditation suffers, because we have not come to the meditation cushion in a suitable frame of mind. If we have been letting go all day, the mind is ready and can now let go in meditation too. Then it can experience its own happiness and purity.

Sometimes people think of the teaching as a sort of therapy, which it undoubtedly is, but that is not its ultimate aim. The Buddha's teaching takes us to the end of our suffering once and for all, not just momentarily when things go wrong.

Having had an experience of letting go, even just once, proves beyond a shadow of a doubt that we carry around a great burden of hate and greed. When we drop this heavy load, we free ourselves from the duality of judgment. It is pleasant to be without thinking, for mental formations are troublesome.

If we succeed even once or twice a day to let go of our reactions, we have taken a great step. We have realized with relief that a feeling that has arisen need not be carried around all day. Our relief proves that we have made a great inner discovery and that the simplicity of nonduality takes us toward truth.

16

Our Underlying Tendencies

ꝛ *M*ost people are inclined to blame themselves or others for what they dislike. Some people like to blame others, some prefer to blame themselves. Neither is profitable or brings peace of mind.

It may help us to get a grip on human reality if we see the underlying tendencies *(anusaya)* within us. If we understand that every human being has these tendencies, we may be less inclined to take offense and blame others and more inclined to accept whatever happens with equanimity. We may be more prone to work on our negativities when we realize they are a universal human affliction.

The underlying tendencies are more subtle than the five hindrances. The five hindrances are gross and manifest themselves as such. They are: sensual desire, wanting that which is pleasing to the senses; ill will, getting angry and upset; sloth and torpor, having no energy whatsoever (sloth refers to the body, torpor to the mind); restlessness and worry, being ill at ease and unpeaceful; skeptical doubt, not knowing which way to turn. These five are easily discernible in ourselves and others. But the underlying tendencies are more difficult to pinpoint. Their roots are deeply imbedded and therefore hard to see and eliminate. They are the hidden sources of the hindrances, and to get rid of them we need keen mindfulness and a great deal of discernment.

Having worked with the five hindrances and let go of their grossest aspects, we can begin work on the underlying tendencies. The first two tendencies, sensuality and irritation, are similar to the hindrances of sensual desire and anger, for which they are the underlying basis. Even when sensual desire has been largely abandoned and anger no longer arises, the dispositions to sensuality and irritation remain.

Sensuality shows itself when we become attached and react to what we see, hear, smell, taste, touch, and think. We are concerned with what we feel and have not yet understood that sense objects are only impermanent phenomena arising and passing away. When we lack this profound insight, we ascribe importance to the sense impressions. We are drawn to them and seek pleasure in them. Humans are sensual beings. There is a verse that describes the Noble Sangha as having "pacified senses." The *Loving-Kindness Discourse* describes the ideal monk as "with senses calmed." In many a discourse the Buddha said that getting rid of sense desire is the way to nibbāna.

Sensuality has to be transcended with great effort and insight. It is impossible to succeed just by avowing, "Sensuality isn't useful, I'll let go of it." One has to gain the insight that these sense contacts have no intrinsic value in themselves. There is an impinging of the sense base (eye, ear, nose, tongue, skin, mind) with the sense object (sight, sound, smell, taste, touch, thought) and the sense consciousness (seeing, hearing, smelling, tasting, touching, thinking). That is all that happens. As long as we react to these contacts as if they had importance, sensuality and irritation arise—the two go hand in hand. Sensuality is satisfied when the sense contact is pleasant. Irritation arises when the sense contact is unpleasant. Irritation does not have to be expressed as anger, shouting, fury, hate, or even resistance. It is just irritation, which results in being displeased, feeling ill at ease and restless. It goes together with being a sensuous human being.

Sensuality and irritation disappear only for the nonreturner *(anāgāmī)*, who is the last stage before full enlightenment and does not return to this realm, but attains nibbāna in the "pure abodes." Even the stream-enterer *(sotāpanna)* and the once-returner *(sakadāgāmī)*, who are at the first and second stages of noble attainment, are still beset by the dukkha of sensuality and irritation.

So long as we imagine that the impulse behind sensuality or irritation is outside of ourselves, we have not seen the beginning of the path. We must realize that our reactions are our own; only then will we start to work on ourselves. If we do not even notice where our reactions come from, how can we do anything about them? Since they occur constantly, we have innumerable occasions to become aware of our inner world.

Becoming aware in and of itself does not get rid of our reactions. We must recognize that getting upset with our reactivity is a futile, unwholesome response. When we see that sensuality and irritation are underlying tendencies that create sensual desire and ill will, this insight should arouse in us some tolerance of our own difficulties and those of other people. What is there to get upset about? The only thing to do is to work with these mind states by taking them as subjects for contemplation and introspection. It is well worthwhile to use our difficulties as a method of purification.

Our tendencies and hindrances are all interconnected. If we are able to diminish even one, the others also become a little less obstructive, lose their heaviness, and cease to be so frightening. People generally fear their own reactions. That is why we often feel threatened by others—we are less afraid of what the other person will say or do than of how we will react. We are unsure of ourselves, afraid of becoming aggressive or angry and thereby diminishing our own self-image.

Having a self-image is detrimental to insight, because it is based on the illusion of permanence. Everything constantly changes, including ourselves, while a self-image presupposes stability. One moment we may be a sensual being, the next moment an irritable one. Sometimes we are at ease, at other times we are restless. Who are we? Any permanent image of ourselves can never have a basis in fact. Such an image will block our insight into the underlying tendencies, blinding us to those that do not fit.

The third underlying tendency is doubt or hesitation. If we have doubts, we hesitate: What am I going to do next? Worrying about our path and abilities, we do not use our time wisely. At times we may waste it or overindulge in activities without benefit. We are obsessed by uncertainty and insecurity. We are afraid of not being safe. But there is no safety anywhere but nibbāna. If we pay attention to our fears and insecurities, we can move beyond them and accomplish so much more.

Doubt and hesitation are abandoned with stream-entry. The one who has attained this first supermundane path and fruit no longer doubts. Having personally experienced an unconditioned reality that is totally different from the relative reality in which we live, the stream-enterer can forge ahead without worry or fear. There can be no doubt about a direct experience. If we tell a small child, "Please don't touch the stove, you might get burned," the child may nevertheless touch the stove. Having once touched it and experienced the pain of being burned, however, she will surely never touch it again. Actual experience removes doubt and hesitation.

The next underlying tendency is the wrong view (diṭṭhi) of relating all that happens to a self. This goes on constantly in us all. Very few of us realize, "This is just a mental phenomenon." Instead we believe: "I think this." When there is pain in the body, few of us say, "It's just an unpleasant feeling." Instead we say, "I'm not feeling very good," or "I have a bad pain." This portrayal of whatever happens as revolving around a "self" is a tendency so deeply imbedded that it takes great effort to uproot.

Abandoning the wrong view of self does not follow from the simple intellectual understanding that there is no real self. It requires an inner view of this whole conglomeration of mind and body as nothing but mere phenomena without ownership. The first step is taken at stream-entry, when the right view of self arises, though all clinging to self-concepts is abandoned only at the arahant level.

Next comes pride or conceit (māna), which here means having a certain concept of ourselves, such as being a man or a woman, young or old, beautiful or ugly. We conceive of what we want, feel, think, know, own, and do. All this conceptualizing creates ownership, and we become proud of possessions, knowledge, skills, feelings, being someone special. This pride may be deeply hidden and need some introspective digging, since it involves our whole being. When someone says to us: "Now find that concept about being a woman," our answer often is, "Of course, I am a woman, what else?" But as long as *I* am anything—woman, man, child, stupid, or intelligent—*I* am far from nibbāna. Whatever I conceptualize myself to be stops me in my tracks.

The underlying tendency of pride and conceit is uprooted only in the arahant. Māna has no directly discernible relationship to any of the hindrances, but, like diṭṭhi, it is a chief manifestation of delusion, the root cause for all our defilements.

Next we come to clinging to existence (bhavarāga). That is our survival syndrome. We cling to being here, unwilling to give up, not ready to die today. We must learn to be ready to die now—which does not mean wishing to die but rather accepting death as an ever present possibility. Wishing to die is the other side of the coin of clinging to existence. It is trying to get rid of "me" because life is too difficult. But being ready to die now means seeing the fallacy in clinging to being someone, and abandoning it.

Clinging to existence leads us into dependency. We want everything to work out well for us, and we resent it if that does not happen. This creates irritation and sensuality. We often forget that we are only guests here on this planet. Our visit is limited and can be over at any time. Clinging to being alive projects us into the future, so that we cannot attend to the present. There is no life in the future, it is all ideation, conjecture, a hope, and a prayer. If we really want to be alive and experience things as they are, we have to be here now, attending to each moment. This entails letting go of clinging to what will happen to us in the future, particularly the question of whether we will continue to exist. Existing in this moment is enough. Then there will be strong mindfulness, real attention, and clear knowing.

Clinging to existence always give us the idea that something better is coming along if we just wait long enough, which discourages effort. Effort must be made now. Who knows what tomorrow will bring?

The last of the seven tendencies is ignorance (avijjā): ignoring the Four Noble Truths. We disregard reality by not realizing that all our dukkha comes from desire, even if our desire is a wholesome one. If we continue to ignore the first two Noble Truths, not to speak of the third, which is nibbāna, we stay enmeshed in dukkha. Our underlying tendency of ignorance yields the wrong view of self—the conceiving of a "self"—without which there would be no sensuality or irritation, no hesitation or doubt, no wrong view, no pride or conceit, and no clinging to existence.

In our practice, it is very useful to pick an underlying tendancy that creates much difficulty for us and make it our focus of attention. Since all the tendencies are interconnected, minimizing one will help to reduce the others.

To see these underlying tendencies in ourselves takes a great deal of proper attention, which requires time and solitude. We cannot do it while talking with others. If the mind is clear, we can do it during meditation sessions or through contemplation.

Contemplation is a valid adjunct to meditation, an important helpmate always directed toward insight, while meditation may alternately be geared toward serenity. Contemplation means looking inward and trying to see what arises: What makes me tick? With utter truthfulness, bring to mind the underlying tendencies, recall that everybody has them, and ask: How are they manifesting in me? Once we have discovered this, we can contemplate further: How can I get rid of this particular tendency, or at least minimize it? We can allot some time during each day to contemplation. Then, when we sit down to meditate, we will find it easier to go inward.

17

Sorrowless, Stainless, and Secure

*S*orrowless, stainless, and secure are three ways of describing an arahant. To be sorrowless means to be without dukkha; to be stainless, without defilements; and to be secure, without fear. Obviously these three are extremely desirable, as they make for peace and happiness. When we learn that they are characteristics of an arahant, we may well wonder whether we should even dream of achieving them. We may consider them beyond our reach.

We all know what it is like to be sorrowful, stained, and insecure. We encounter dukkha repeatedly. We see our defilements whenever we get upset, worried, anxious, envious, or jealous. And we have all experienced fear: fear of our own death or that of our loved ones, fear of not being liked, praised, and accepted, or fear of not reaching our goals or of making fools of ourselves.

We can also experience the opposites of those three defiled states. If the seeds did not lie within us, enlightenment would be a myth. When we have a really concentrated meditation, dukkha does not arise. No defilements can enter because the mind is occupied—not with defilements but with its object of concentration, which is wonderful even if it lasts for only a single moment. There can be no fear because all is well. Concentration in meditation brings an inner joy and peacefulness that have nothing to do with outer conditions; they are strictly factors of the mind. We cannot cultivate them successfully if we neglect them during those hours when we are not meditating. We need to guard and protect the mind from evil thoughts at all times.

The more often we experience these moments of being sorrowless, stainless, and secure, the more they become part of us. When we acknowledge

Mature Practice

꒜

18

Relating to Oneself

*T*he *Loving-Kindness Discourse* explains how we should behave toward other people—we should treat them as our own children. But it doesn't say anything about how we should behave toward ourselves. Yet we treat ourselves the way we treat others.

Since we are all primarily concerned with ourselves, it is very important that we have an idea of what we are confronting. It's only an illusion that, through the presence of other people, we confront the world around us. In reality, we are constantly meeting our own inner defilements or strengths. What goes on around us serves only as a series of triggers for our reactions.

The world around us consists of situations, experiences, and people that we contact through our senses. The strongest of the senses is the mind with its thinking capacity. Thoughts, unfortunately, have a tendency to fly off the handle. We don't usually pay attention to what *is* because we are interested in what we think might be. We either fear the future or hope for the best. Our hopes are wishful thinking, and our fears are unfounded worries. Both create turmoil. Our hopes give rise to fear—fear that our hopes might not be realized. And our fears give rise to hope—the hope that if we just act cleverly enough, what we fear won't materialize. Then again, we're afraid that we might not measure up to handle all that will confront us.

Consequently we find ourselves feeling tense and uneasy, feelings which we relieve through diverse distractions: food, drink, entertainment, talk, sleep, newspapers, television, telephones—whatever we can find. If nothing is available, we get depressed or upset.

In reality all our diversifications (papañca) started because the mind gave itself the liberty to be out of control. We allow it to go in all directions, thinking of the future with fear or hope, thinking of the past with regret or sentimentality, instead of attending to what is really happening.

Being attentive to the moment is the meaning of mindfulness. Perfect mindfulness is difficult because of the mind's tendency to proliferate. Were we perfectly attentive to each moment, none of this proliferation would happen. But we need to do more than remind ourselves to be mindful. We need some kind of aid. One emotional support we can use is appreciation for ourselves. Appreciation does not imply a feeling of superiority in which we enumerate all the things we know. There may be a big gap between what we know and what we do. But it is very helpful to consider what we have done. Nothing really matters besides our actions. What we know is immaterial, but what we actually do has consequences. If we want to have an attitude of appreciation for ourselves, we need to remember our wholesome actions.

We also need to be content with ourselves, otherwise we will never be content anywhere, with anything or anybody. We are stuck with this "me" for the time being—stuck with both a great obstacle and a great teacher. Our foremost priority lies in finding contentment with ourselves as we are, so that we can then recognize positive fundamental human qualities. This is well brought out in the *Loving-Kindness Discourse,* which says that we should be content and easily satisfied. The discourse mentions fifteen conditions that bring peacefulness. If we can't find these qualities within ourselves, inner peace will evade us.

Being content means being satisfied with what we own and with how we look, speak, live, and react. Everything needs to have an air of contentment about it. That doesn't mean that we can't improve. But if we feel a serious lack in ourselves, this will color our attitudes and reactions. There will always be the tension of wanting something else. The more we let go of wanting, the more we let go of dukkha. But to do that, we need to be content with what there is, even if it is not exactly what we expect. Everybody has expectations of themselves and of others, but they are unrealistic. They do not take impermanence into account. Everything constantly changes. Something may have been perfectly all right a moment ago, but now it's not. How can we feel content in situations that we consider unsatisfactory? First of all, we can check out the situation a little more closely. Why isn't it satisfactory? What's lacking? Not enough ego affirmation? Not what we expected? Once we see why something is unsatisfactory, we will find it trifling, not even worth considering.

When something creates dukkha within us again and again, arousing the tension of ungratified desire, we should reflect, "I am of the nature to die, I have not gone beyond death." Why not keep death in mind? Recollection of death is neither morbid nor depressing, and it brings us a little nearer to reality. Would we react with discontent if we knew we only had another ten minutes to live? If we really had only ten more minutes to live, none of our reactions would be discontented. There might be fear, which arises out of hate, but what is the use of hating something inevitable? Why should anyone hate anything that is going to happen, for that matter? It's one of our innumerable absurdities.

Contentment includes appreciation of ourselves. When everything around us seems to create havoc and turmoil, we can return to an inner feeling of goodness and beauty. If we didn't have the basis for purity within us, there wouldn't be much sense in practicing. We can, however, enlarge and cultivate our inner purity and develop our awareness of it. Whenever there is turmoil and fear, dislike or dukkha from an unfulfilled desire, we can always return to our center, where contentment lies.

We have the mistaken notion that contentment is dependent upon certain conditions or people. How can it be dependent upon something outside of ourselves? If we want true contentment, it has to depend on what lies within us. Then we can arouse it again and again. If we depend on people or situations for our contentment, we become a slave to them. But the Buddha's path is the way to freedom.

Like contentment, a sense of gratitude is of great help in our lives. It does not have to be directed toward anyone or anything in particular. It can be thankfulness for the karmic conditions that have made real effort possible, or for having a body in fairly good condition. It means not taking anything positive for granted. The richer people are, the more they accept their privilege as a matter of course. The more health or opportunities we have, the more we take them for granted. That is not conducive to contentment. Gratitude for these blessings creates contentment.

Unless we have the right kind of attitude, a feeling of being at home with ourselves, of being able to rest and relax within, we will not be at home anywhere. Home is where the heart is, not where the body is. When the heart opens up and creates a feeling of appreciation, gratitude, contentment, and ease with oneself, then we feel secure and can be at home anywhere on earth, or anywhere in the universe.

Home is not just a house with four walls. A good home should be warm, especially when the world outside seems cold. Where can warmth be, if not in our hearts? This is where we have to create the comfort, the happiness, the elusive peace for which we search. The heart is our center. When things go smoothly, we take them as our due. But when difficulties confront us, we look around for outside help, although help is actually to be found within our hearts. That help is always there, if we have created a secure, warm, and loving foundation within.

Depending on others for happiness is foolish, relying on them for security is absurd. How could we depend on someone who is also just trying to find happiness and security? Only the person who has found this inner wealth has a good home. Centering on our own happiness and security enables us to withstand all kinds of turmoil and difficulties. Nobody in this world gets away without dukkha, and only if we have found our center do we know where to go in times of crisis. These crises may be relatively small: perhaps many people are talking at once or demanding something of us, or maybe some of our expectations are unfulfilled. So we enter into our hearts, where we find warmth, appreciation, gratitude, and contentment. We learn to do this by dropping every single unwholesome thought, so that only skillful, beneficial, and positive mind states remain. The more unwholesome thoughts we have, the more our home, the heart, becomes defiled and unpleasant. Once we have dropped a thought, we gain the strength to drop it again. By doing so we clean up our home. We sweep our rooms and hallways. Let's sweep the heart every day!

Whenever we clean up something—an overgrown garden, the kitchen floor, our dirty laundry—we should remember to clean our hearts at the same time. When we have a clean, solid base inside the heart, we feel love for ourselves, which produces a similar feeling for our environment. Then we need no longer *try* to be nice to others; acting nicely is a natural outcome of being nice to ourselves. Being nice to ourselves never means being indulgent. It means cultivating love for ourselves, which makes it easy to be loving toward others.

Others benefit from our solidity. We become an anchor, a rock that others can use. Whatever happens, we remain solid and unshaken.

When we have warmth and security in the heart, our meditation benefits and our life takes on a different texture. It feels as if we were living a fractured life before, and now we are healed and whole. The holy life means becoming whole, of one piece.

19

Tender Loving Care

Have you heard the expression "TLC"—tender loving care? Babies cannot thrive without it, nor can we. We know that if babies and small children are deprived of tenderness and love, all the best food and medicine will not make them grow properly. Relationships don't thrive without TLC. How could meditation flourish without it?

We must give our mind tender loving care and not let it become a bull in a china shop, whose careless, impulsive actions wreak havoc. Carelessness in even the smallest detail indicates a lack of love. Whenever we do not comply with even a small detail of the precepts, we are not caring for ourselves.

The precepts are not arbitrary. Each precept is designed for a particular purpose. Their overall aim is to remove us from mundane concerns and turn our attention inward. Any precept that we do not uphold lovingly and tenderly will disrupt our meditation. Even the slightest deviation from a precept will be disruptive, because it will allow the mind to follow its disobedient and careless habits. Such a mind will not develop a loving regard for others, and meditation will suffer accordingly. When the mind is heedless during the day, how can we expect it to be attentive during meditation? Meditation can flourish only if we use the mind in the right way all day long, and also have tender loving care for the meditation itself. We have to sit down and give ourselves gracefully to the situation, with a feeling of love toward everything.

In Zen practice, before one sits down one makes a bow to the meditation cushion and to the person opposite. This nice gesture expresses respect and care for one's surroundings, for all that comes within one's focus of attention. We can also think loving and caring thoughts about the breath before we start.

A mind full of doubts and regrets, resistances, worries, or judgments can't possibly meditate. It doesn't stop resisting, worrying, or judging just because we have sat down on a pillow.

There is only one way to meditate successfully: by turning away from mundane concerns. Meditation is a transcending activity, which cannot be done with worldly mind states. As long as worldly concerns beckon us and promise some sort of satisfaction, we cannot establish a transcendental consciousness. Every time worldly thoughts arise during the day, we can examine whether they have ever brought lasting contentment. If the answer is no we can drop them more easily.

Any task can be done as part of practice by using utter mindfulness, one-pointed attention without judgment. We need not determine whether this task is necessary and important or whether it is difficult, cumbersome, and tedious. All we need to do is pay attention to what's happening and offer tender loving care to ourselves for doing our best. Take, for example, the task of cleaning our room. If we have tender loving care while cleaning our room and attending our daily duties, then we can have the same care and love in the heart when we sit down to meditate. Why should there be any difference between these two actions?

The mind has accumulated habits for many years. If we recognize them, we can learn to substitute new and better ones. We can think in terms of loving and serving others. We can remember universal suffering and the impermanence of all that has arisen. By bringing these teachings into the mind as often as possible, we point the mind in the right direction and get it out of its old grooves.

If we love what we are doing, we will do it well; otherwise we have little chance of succeeding. Resistance and rejection, or at least indifference, will block the path. As far as our meditation is concerned, we need to choose our attitude carefully, with wisdom and compassion for ourselves.

A mind that hasn't yet matured is like a baby. It needs to be handled carefully. As long as we haven't glimpsed liberation—nibbāna—we must treat our fragile mind considerately. We should never abuse it by having anger, hate, resistance, rejection, worry or fear, dislike or doubt; rather, we should love every aspect of life, whether it produces comfort or discomfort.

If we don't handle the mind carefully, it won't grow, and our practice is all about growing up, maturing. Maturity of mind is not dependent upon age but upon the training we do, both in meditation and in life (how can we separate the two?).

Unless we give ourselves utterly to what we are doing, there cannot be a wholehearted endeavor. We cannot pick and choose. If we pick one thing and not another, we create separation. We must not pick and choose the people we want to love, or the teachings we want to remember, or the precepts that we would like to keep. Every time we reject, dismiss, or ignore someone or something, we block our meditation. Every person has to be loved, everything that is going on has to be attended to, every precept has to be cared for.

If the mind is not wholeheartedly involved and without resistance, it will function only halfheartedly. Maybe it likes the first twenty minutes of meditation and doesn't appreciate the subsequent forty minutes. Maybe it likes to concentrate on the breath and doesn't like it when somebody coughs.

Successful meditation is an incentive, almost a bribe: "If I behave myself all day long, I'll have a good meditation at night." Nobody knows how our minds behave. Only we do. The mind is the only instrument that makes everything possible, from the basest desires and actions to the highest levels of consciousness. But we must remember to be caring and recognize everything that happens as part and parcel of practice.

If we love our breath, it will be much easier to stay with it. That which we love has a magnetic quality. What we don't care about arouses no interest in us. We can love the breath because it is our meditation subject, and love our cushion because it supports us while meditating. We can love the people who meditate with us and be grateful to them. Tender loving care makes everything flourish, from tiny little seeds to minds that enter the jhānas (meditative absorptions) and let go of self.

20

Stretching the Mind to the Impossible

*W*e usually limit ourselves in all we do by imagining that things are impossible or that we are limited in what we can accomplish. We do this in all spheres but especially in the spiritual life. If we could let go of the idea of the impossible and drop our petty considerations—our likes and dislikes, our worries and fears, our resistances—we would open up to the flow of experience.

We are aware of only a small percentage of all that exists in this universe. What we perceive through the senses is a fraction of the whole. Bees can see ultraviolet light, which we can't. Dogs can hear sounds so high pitched that they are beyond our hearing range. These beings' reasoning processes are much less developed than ours, but their senses can pick up sights and sounds beyond our capacity. These are just a few examples of how full our universe is of experiences and possibilities of which we have no inkling. When we dismiss these possibilities, we limit ourselves greatly.

We are better acquainted with scientific technology than with spiritual development. Scientific technology is our birthright. Fifty years ago it was considered impossible to go to the moon, almost a joke. If the scientists who finally managed to build a rocket to reach the moon hadn't thought it possible, they could not have succeeded. Now, not even a lifetime later, we accept space exploration as a matter of course. A seemingly impossible proposal became actual.

Something analogous happens in spiritual life and meditation. Nobody can place limits on our meditation, our spiritual cultivation, or our aspirations. Nothing is stopping us from achieving anything—nothing other than our belief that we face insurmountable obstacles. But if we turn that around and think of what we *can* do, the impossible becomes possible. Nothing is beyond our capacities in life, or in meditation. We can concentrate and become absorbed in other states of consciousness, once we let go of the barriers that keep us from flowing into each moment.

We need to give in to the unknown and give up old, habitual reactions. Giving in and giving up are the most essential parts of making meditation work. We give in to the breath and give up the whole conglomeration of thoughts, which have no factual basis anyway. The only facts are impermanence (anicca), nonfulfillment (dukkha), and corelessness (anattā). Everything else is ideation, personal opinion. If the mind is full of the ideas that one has elaborated and verbalized during the day, how can there be room for concentration, for blissfulness, peace, and insight? If we allow the mind to spout ideas constantly, how can it stop suddenly when we sit down for meditation?

There is something far beyond what we know. Our longing for fulfillment directs our search for transcendence. If we did not have this longing, we would never be able to endure our physical discomforts and continue our practice. Nobody needs to tell us that there is more to human life than what we have experienced. We know there is more, because deep, inner contentment has escaped us so far.

We need to give the mind a good, solid stretch. We need to reach an entirely different realm, one in which worldly concerns are left behind. We do not abandon our everyday duties, responsibilities, and activities, but we are unaffected by their results. We can still water our flowers, cook meals, type letters, or sew robes. These are worldly actions, done as a matter of course, but the mind stays free and clear. It remains sorrowless, stainless, and secure. In the *Great Blessings Discourse* the arahants are described in this way: "Though touched by worldly circumstance, never are their minds wavering. Stainless, sorrowless, and secure, theirs is the highest blessing." This doesn't mean that one can't look after worldly things, but an expanded, unobstructed mind has a different inner vision. Attaining this vision requires much resolution, for we need to be able to drop everything. We hear the sound of a firecracker, but we drop the idea that it is a firecracker. Much strength of mind and sustained determination are needed for that. But unless we arouse such strength—and devotion and love for our practice—we are wasting valuable time, and meditation will be only a hope and a prayer.

In the description of the meditative absorptions (jhāna) that the Buddha gives in his discourses, the first word is always "secluded." Secluding the mind means protecting it, watching it, giving it a place where it can expand and unfold. Nothing unfolds to its advantage unless it is sheltered, so it can grow and mature.

We need to be caring and considerate of our inner being, watch it carefully, protect it like a precious jewel, so that it does not get battered and scratched. A mind with scratches can't meditate. When we protect our minds from unwholesome and unnecessary activity, meditation becomes much easier. We protect our bodies, as best we can, from getting burned, scratched, hit, or hurt. When an accident happens, we enlist the help of a first aid kit, a doctor, or a hospital. Yet we let the mind get burned, scratched, and abraded by its ego assertions and reactions, and afflicted with worldly considerations of like and dislike, anger and rejection. These ideas scratch at the pure texture of the mind. If we wound the mind often enough—and nobody's immune from that—scratches become deep scars, difficult to heal. These scars are our limitations. The mind is a jewel, beautiful in its purity. Scarring and scratching it brings unhappiness.

Only we can protect our mind. Only we can prevent the negative thoughts that scratch the jewel of the mind. When we truly work for our inner purification, we need no longer blame outside conditions for our reactions. We are the guardians and cultivators of the mind. We can compare our mind to a wide open field to which little has been done except for some planting of seeds and some scratching here and there, which has left scarring. As we become aware of the good seeds, we can cultivate them.

Cultivating the mind takes time, patience, goodwill, and determination. If we fail to cultivate the mind we find ourselves in the same situation over and over again, thinking instead of concentrating. We continue to get upset about all sorts of matters that are, when looked at dispassionately, quite petty. We completely overlook the totality of existence, the imminence of death, the attainment of a consciousness that goes beyond all duality, and the possibility of attaining freedom beyond grief and suffering.

A mind concerned only with worldly matters is a shrunken mind, with limited horizons. We need a flexible and malleable mind, one that encompasses all that exists. We have been cultivating worldly mental processes for lifetimes, year after year, day in and day out—we need not continue. We are perfectly capable of feeding, dressing, washing ourselves, and working at our jobs. We don't have to develop these abilities any further. We're very fortunate to have done all that already. Now the time has come to cultivate an expanded mind, to let go of obstructions, to stretch the mind toward impeccable peace. The key is letting go. When all other thoughts have been released, wisdom arises and peace settles in the heart and mind.

Sorrow, pain, grief, and lamentation are all defilements. There is no rationale behind any of them. When the Buddha was dying, Ānanda, his attendant, was only a stream-enterer, the lowest of the four types of noble disciples. Ānanda was grieving. Other monks, all arahants, were sitting quietly, awaiting the event. The Buddha called Ānanda over and asked him, "What are you crying about? Are you crying over this old body that is being discarded?" Ānanda said, "I am crying about losing my teacher, who was compassionately showing me the way." The Buddha replied, "I have told you everything that is necessary to attain enlightenment. There's nothing hidden. All you have to do is practice with diligence."

The whole of the teaching goes in one direction only, which means we don't have to worry about choices. We often spend time trying to figure out the best way to practice. This can give rise to debate, argument, and doubt, all of which waste energy that we could use more profitably for spiritual endeavors.

If we come to the meditation pillow with a childlike mind, we will find it easier to forget the world. We need childlike trust in the impossible. Children believe in Santa Claus, in fairies, little gnomes, and all sorts of impossible things. That's the kind of trust we need to get anywhere with our meditation. We need freedom from skepticism, from trying to find rational answers, from wanting to be clever. Only wisdom will work, and that arises out of a pure heart. There is truly nothing important to keep in mind. If we find something worth remembering, we can write it down so we won't forget it and then come back to paying attention to each moment.

When we begin meditation unaffected by external conditions, completely open, with the conviction that we can do it, then the mind will respond favorably. We can enter a different realm of understanding and awareness and develop the mental capacity needed for the spiritual life. We must trust our own purity without niggling self-doubts or exaggerated expectations.

Sometimes we may be suspicious of our own and other people's abilities, about the teacher, the teaching, or the daily program. Subconsciously there's a disturbance that says, "I think I could do it better." By all means do it better. Trust yourself and love your efforts.

Meditation can be our most wonderful experience, but we have to make it so. The Buddha's teaching goes into human psychology in extraordinary depth; the ordinary mind cannot grasp its full impact. Unless the mind becomes *extra*ordinary through meditation, we cannot possibly gain the understanding that the Buddha expounded. The ordinary mind does not have the depth, lucidity, and expansion necessary for such transcendental wisdom.

Full meditative absorptions are the means to an end, namely insight. If the mind cannot become one-pointed, insight will not arise. The mind will remain contracted, dull, hampered by obstructions. Our full potential arises when we can direct our minds at all times to wherever we wish. Only then does the totality of anicca, dukkha, and anattā become an inner reality.

Until the reactions and obstructions have been removed from the mind, there will be no room for new realizations. Our understanding of the Buddha's teaching will be limited by the boundaries we have erected. Meditation removes the limitations, widens our horizons, and deepens our perspective. We can believe in the impossible just as children do and trust in the seed of enlightenment in our hearts.

21

Renunciation

ॐ **I**n order to embrace the spiritual path fully, to walk on it with a feeling of security, we have to renounce. Renunciation does not necessarily mean cutting off one's hair or wearing robes. It means letting go of ideas and hopes that the mind wants to grasp, to keep, to investigate. The mind always wants to have more. If it cannot get more, it makes up fantasies and projects them upon the world. All this will never bring true satisfaction and inner peace, which can be won only by renunciation. "Letting go," the fading away of desire, is a key element of the Buddhist path. We must realize once and for all that *more* is not *better*. It is impossible to come to an end of *more*. There is always something beyond it. But it is certainly possible to come to the end of *less*.

Why sit in seclusion in meditation and spoil our chances at all the opportunities the world offers for enjoyment? We could go on trips, work at a challenging job, meet interesting people, write letters or read books, have a pleasant time somewhere else, and really feel at ease—we could even find a different spiritual path. When our meditation does not succeed, the thought may arise: What am I really doing, and what good is it? Then the idea comes: I can't do this very well, maybe I should try something else.

This glittering world promises us much but never keeps its promises. We have all tried its temptations, but none of them have been truly fulfilling. Real fulfillment—a complete peace that lacks nothing—cannot be found in the world. The world holds nothing that can utterly satisfy one's wants. Money, material possessions, another person, none of these can do so. And yet we have a niggling doubt: Maybe I'll find something else, more comfortable, less demanding, and, above all, new.

The mind has to be understood for what it is—just another sense. It has, as its base, the brain, just as sight has the eyes. As the mind moments arise and contact is made with them, we start believing and even owning what we are thinking. We are greatly concerned with our thoughts and look after them, just as we look after our belongings. Yet they never bring us happiness. What they bring is hope and worry and doubt. Sometimes they entertain us, sometimes they make us depressed. When doubts arise and we go along with them, they can lead us to the point at which there is no practice left at all. Yet the only way to prove that the spiritual life brings fulfillment is to practice, to let go of expectations and desires, so that there is nothing lacking and nothing to fill. The proof of the pudding lies in the eating. Wanting outside proof is the wrong approach.

Looking for fulfillment outside ourselves is a common mistake: "I want to be given knowledge, understanding, loving-kindness, consideration. I want to receive a spiritual awakening." But there is nothing that we can be given, except instructions and methods. We need to do the daily work of practice, so that purification will result. We cannot remedy our lack of fulfillment by being given something new. Where would it come from? From the Buddha? the Dhamma? our teacher? We are not sure. Perhaps we hope to get it from our meditation, or from a book. But the task is not to get something, but to get rid of obstructions.

What do we need to get rid of first? Preferably the convolutions of the mind that tell us fantastic and unbelievable stories. When we hear them, we are apt to believe them. One way to look at them and disbelieve them is to write them down. They sound absurd when we see them on paper. The mind can always think up new stories—there is no end to them. Renunciation is the key. Giving up, letting go.

Giving up also means giving in to that underlying, subconscious knowing that the worldly way does not work, that a different approach is possible. Instead of adding something to our lives, we relinquish our ambitions. (To stay the way we are and add something new—how can that possibly work?) Relinquishing our ambitions means accepting that our old ways of thinking are not useful. Dukkha arises again and again. Sometimes we think, "I must be feeling this way because of him (or her)" or "Maybe it's the weather." Then the weather changes or that person leaves, but dukkha is still there, so we look for some other cause. Instead of wasting our time that way, we need to become pliable and soft and attend to what arises without all the conglomerations and proliferations of the mind. Our mind moments may be pure or impure, and we need to know how to handle both.

Once we start explaining and rationalizing, acceptance is impossible. We must not think that we need to add something to ourselves in order to become complete. We have to discard all our identifications. Then we become a whole person.

The human being always wants something: "I want to be understood, appreciated, loved, praised." Or: "I want to get, buy, experience." Wanting never results in peacefulness. We've been wanting things from the moment we were born. We've never really gotten what we wanted, but we insist on continuing to want anyway.

We can eventually find fulfillment by not wanting. We let go, again and again, of our ideas and opinions. We renounce whoever it is we consider ourselves to be, which is imbedded in our identification process: "I'm all right, look at me, I'm doing fine." Maybe we are all right and doing fine, but as long as total ease and peace are absent, there is something missing. When we say, "I'm doing fine" it suggests that we are trying to refute something. Otherwise we would not be saying it at all.

Our renunciation has to extend into meditation, otherwise we will not succeed. We must give ourselves completely to whatever we are doing in order to have the best results. There must be no question in our minds whether there is something better or more worthwhile to do.

Unless we are wholeheartedly involved with our meditation, it will be a miserable relationship. "Wholeheartedly" means that we give our time, love, and energy unstintingly. Otherwise we are just dabbling. Wholehearted involvement in meditation also means giving in to the meditation subject and giving up our ideas about how it should be done, about what some teachers said, about what we have read. All this has to be discarded so that we can be utterly involved with our meditation only. Then we experience the softness of nonresistance, of just being there and keeping the meditation subject in mind. When there is concentrated absorption, eventually deep insight will arise and with it a chance to get rid of dukkha.

The wholehearted relationship we must have with all experiences extends from eating our food to paying attention to the person sitting next to us, to doing a job, to meditating. When we are wholeheartedly involved, success is bound to come. But in order to be so singleminded we have to give up our ego assertions. When we are concerned with our ego, a complete merging is impossible. Total involvement can be likened to dissolving milk in water—they blend completely. The ego cannot dissolve into the meditation subject; it remains separate.

We also need to renounce our ideas about where we might find happiness, how the spiritual life should be lived, how we should meditate, and how teachers should talk and act. Mindfulness means knowing without judgment. Once I heard a Thai monk, whose English was limited, say, "Knowing only, knowing only." I could not figure out what he meant until one day it dawned on me that he was explaining pure mindfulness.

"Knowing only" implies giving in and giving up. Hanging on to ideas, beliefs, or views is an obstacle. We relate completely to the moment without ideation, here and now.

There is no way that a relationship can work unless heart and mind are both involved. There must be a loving feeling and an understanding. Unless both arise in meditation, real concentration cannot happen. We may sit on the cushion year after year, yet our practice will not flourish. The deliberate mind movement of giving up has to precede the meditation. Otherwise ego will get in the way. It will rear its ugly head and say, "I know better. There are other ways to meditate." The ego will insist on comfort: "I don't feel comfortable, so this must not be right. I'd like something more pleasant."

Unless we learn to renounce all wanting and resistance every time we sit on the cushion, the spiritual path will remain an utter mystery. The Buddha's teaching leads in one direction only—the total elimination of self-delusion. To get there, we have to work on ourselves, little by little, all the time.

Renunciation means letting go of ideation, letting go of the mind-stuff that claims to be the one who knows. Who knows this one who knows? These are only ideas churning around, arising and ceasing. Renunciation is not an outward manifestation. It is an inward movement, one that we need to practice. Meditation cannot happen without it.

22

Emptying the Heart

ॐ One of the things that most of us find extremely difficult, though it sounds easy enough, is to love ourselves. Many of us see a lot of unlovable qualities in ourselves. Quite frequently we recognize these qualities more easily in other people, and we react with resistance and rejection, which results in dissatisfaction with life in general. Rejection of this or that aspect in a person brings nothing but unhappiness to our hearts. These states of mind then turn against us. This is a very unsatisfactory way of relating—it will never generate peacefulness or concentration.

The solution is not to find a different set of friends or to drown out our feelings but rather to think differently, to have a totally new concept of what people actually are. The Buddha was called a "teacher of tameable men." The untamed in us is our ego. Many of those who haven't undergone any training do not see how they constantly act out their desires and dislikes, how they follow their own preoccupations without consideration for anyone else. Others are well aware of their ego preoccupations and yet can't do anything about them, because the taming process hasn't begun yet. Although they are aware of the untamed—their spontaneous instinctive reactivity—they are unable to stop it. Then there are those who are starting to tame themselves. It is a mistake to look at people subjectively, as if their personalities were static and stable. All people except arahants are untamed, but all can be tamed, if they wish. Our attitude toward others should be to see if they are willing to be tamed and disregard all that remains untamed.

Our expectations are responsible for the negative judgments we have about ourselves and others. We do not necessarily expect to be exceptionally good, clever, beautiful, rich, peaceful, or spiritual, but we are adamant about having a solid, firm, and secure ego. This is one of the reasons why amassing material possessions is so popular. The more we have, the more we believe we are somebody, as if having and being were identical. Our search is really for security, and when we can't find it dissatisfaction follows.

We also expect to find contentment through our identifications as a woman or man, as a mother or daughter, as a meditator, or as someone who is clever, worthy, irresponsible, good looking, etc. Although we are again seeking security, others cannot support us, since it is impossible for them to know how we identify ourselves. Since they cannot affirm us, our expectations go unfulfilled. Again dissatisfaction arises, and loving ourselves becomes ever more difficult.

We also hope to become someone more worthy than we are now. Since such a hope entails the future and therefore cannot be fulfilled now, dissatisfaction finds another foothold in our hearts. Anything that is meant to support our ego affirmation will never fulfill us because it exists one moment and vanishes the next. Instead of being happy and peaceful we experience tension and fear—the fear of unfulfilled expectations and the tension of trying to reach fulfillment.

When we identify with any of the five khandhas—body, feeling, perception, mental formations, or consciousness—we suffer. The khandhas have at least some substance; they truly exist. All other identifications, possessions, or attempts to become something, however, are fantasies or of little substance. The dukkha they cause is therefore much greater than what we experience through the khandas. The more we identify and the less we are aware of that habit, the more difficult it becomes to have a loving heart. Clinging creates boundaries, discrimination, and judgments, which prevent openness. The less love we have, the more confused we will be—a loving heart and a clear mind support each other. As long as we reject and resist parts of ourselves and others, we cannot feel peace. We may not even be able to imagine what peace is like.

Peacefulness is not the absence of turmoil. Real health is not the absence of disease. Peacefulness is a state of totality in our inner being, when we have let go of ego identification, expectations, tensions, and the fear of not getting what we want, and when we just rest within our own center. The Buddha's teaching points to renunciation, and the path of practice is about letting go—not possessing, not identifying, not wanting.

Peacefulness is not our birthright, we have to work for it. We are born with the roots of greed and hate, but also with those of generosity and non-hate (love). Our effort must be to cultivate the wholesome roots and let go of the others. That work should never be neglected, not even for a single moment.

When we have a loving heart, the interests of other people are as close to us as our own (which is an easy way to check out whether we truly care or not). When we are concerned only with "me" and "mine," the work of opening the heart is of foremost importance, for the mind is confused and foggy when the heart is narrow and cramped. The heart and mind are not separate identities (in the Pali language both are *citta*). Unless we undertake to cultivate both, we are missing one of the most important aspects of the teaching. Purification of feeling brings clarification of mind. We need to purify our ego-centered emotions, our wanting to receive rather than to give, and reject the untamed in ourselves.

The difficulty in loving others is the same as in loving ourselves. Loving ourselves doesn't mean feeling superior, proud, or having exaggerated ideas about our own capacities. It is more a feeling of kindness or motherliness toward ourselves. "Just as a mother at the risk of life loves and protects her child, her only child..." says the *Loving-Kindness Discourse* of the Buddha. If we generate that kind of love for ourselves, we can extend it to others, and a balanced feeling of harmony arises within. Then both meditation and life in general flow more smoothly. When we watch our inner movements not just with an intellectual understanding of arising and ceasing but with deep interest and care, we try to reduce our negativities. This way we will encounter fewer obstacles on our path.

Some renunciation of expectations, attachments, and desires must occur. Wanting something is the cause of dukkha. If we really want to diminish dukkha, we have to work on our desires. A spiritual path is one of inner effort; it is not a matter of simply sitting on a meditation pillow. The real spiritual journey happens when we see what arises in ourselves and are able to let go.

We can usually recognize what motivates others more easily than what motivates us. However, what we see in others is only a reflection of ourselves, otherwise we would not be able to grasp the meaning of what we see. So instead of blaming or disliking the other person, we know what needs to be done: to see that person as a mirror for ourselves. If we can recognize and relate to something happening to someone else, it is because we have experienced it ourselves.

Happiness and peacefulness are synonymous. Happiness and pleasure are opposites. Pleasure is a momentary, short-lived sense contact; happiness is a state of being. If we have no inner happiness, we cannot experience peacefulness. It's essential to find out the reasons for our lack of inner happiness. What is it I'm wanting and not getting? What expectation is not being fulfilled? What am I clinging to in myself or with others? What am I fearful of losing? Am I constantly trying to reaffirm my own image and no one is supporting me? No peacefulness can be found in any of these mind states.

Unless there is a direct knowing of these inner difficulties, we can't do anything about them. The direct knowing arises from introspection, which is *sati*, or mindfulness. This short word includes the way, the path, and the fruit. Mindfulness is directed toward one's inner being, but with the sharpness of a microscope, not with the superficial attention we pay to most things. That clarity is sometimes felt to be painful, for what we find may not be attractive; but the pain here arises from judgment, from a rejection of some aspect of ourselves. We would experience far more pain if we never knew purification.

It's obvious from the Buddha's teachings that the defilements are universal and that purification is possible. In order to tread the path of purification, we need to investigate our desires, even write them down and ask ourselves whether we really want them. Maybe we want to be loved, admired, or appreciated; maybe we want to be very clever or highly realized; or maybe we just want peace. Then the next question is, How are we to find inner peace? When we write down our experiences and reflect on them, we soon see that peacefulness is connected with giving up desires.

It doesn't mean that we can give up all craving and clinging immediately, but we start on the path of renunciation, of letting go. When a desire arises, we look at it, smile, and see it vanish. Instead of desire, generosity arises in the heart. When the heart isn't full of craving, we can fill its spaciousness with love. Love is generosity of the heart. There's nothing else we can do with love except to give it away. When desires diminish, then love and generosity grow. We need never think that loving is dependent on someone who is lovable, for this kind of appreciation or admiration is a type of clinging. Love is a quality of the heart that has nothing to do with the quality of the persons we love.

Letting go—renunciation—allows us to be more loving toward ourselves and others and draws us toward peacefulness. Wanting and desiring, however, with their restless searching and insecurity, create a battleground in the heart and mind. Not wanting cannot create a fear of not getting something or of losing what we have. The tension of these mind states cannot arise, and so we stay centered in the here and now.

If peacefulness is our aim, renunciation must be our path—of this we have no choice. Emptying the heart and mind of desires, of our self-image, of expectations, and of being somebody special, and instead filling them with generosity, will open the door to loving-kindness. Until we actually make that happen, loving-kindness remains a hope and an unfulfilled expectation.

The Buddha did not try to convince anyone of his teachings but suggested that we try to follow his guidelines and see the results for ourselves. This is the Buddha's way: clear-cut and straightforward, and trodden by many over the centuries.

We are not machines, and our human mind is not just a logical computer. Our minds have feelings, with which we are intimately connected. When we hear the Buddha's teachings, it can touch our hearts. We know deep down, without even having experienced the results, that it holds profound truth.

A Glimpse of Liberation

ॐ

23
Liberation Here and Now

*W*hen we hear or read the word "liberation" (nibbāna), we often get the idea that it is unattainable, otherworldly, reachable only by spiritual giants, and that it has very little to do with us. We do not have to look at it that way. Let us consider the three kinds of liberation: "signless," "wishless," and "voidness" liberation. Signless liberation is attained by completely penetrating impermanence (anicca), wishless liberation by completely penetrating unsatisfactoriness (dukkha), and voidness liberation by penetrating coreless substance (anattā).

We're all familiar with impermanence, but what is signless liberation? Suppose we are attached to or highly appreciative of a person, a situation, a belonging. Can we let go of clinging to it? We can try to let go of anything at all, no matter how small. We direct our attention to the fact that all we examine is totally fleeting. We fathom that truth in everything, in all living beings, and, having seen it, we let go of our belief in the solidity of things. We thereby let go of our attachment. If we can do that with anything or anyone, even for a moment, we have won a moment of signless liberation—a moment of direct knowledge that nothing has any intrinsic value, that it's all a passing show. Having had that experience, even for one moment, gives us an inkling of what the Buddha meant when he spoke about freedom.

Freedom is often misunderstood as the ability to do anything we want. We have probably tried that already and found that it doesn't work. Even if we were to follow only our desires, we would soon be satiated and then feel unfulfilled.

Freedom means nonattachment, which is not indifference but rather the penetration of absolute truth. To see that clearly, we let go for one moment of anything that we call our own, anything that we like or consider important. We examine it until its fleeting nature has become quite apparent. Then the moment comes when we can say, "I don't have to have that, I can do without it." That is a moment of truth. Having a moment of truth is always possible, but such moments don't come automatically. We have to inquire into our clinging and work at loosening it. Letting go sounds easy, and it is, but only after it has happened. Before that, it entails much self-examination.

A moment of signless liberation can be experienced in another way. Suppose, for instance, there is an unpleasant feeling in the body that creates a reaction of "I don't want it. Go away now!" When we really penetrate into the impermanence of that feeling—when we see how it has no basic reality or significance and, for just a moment, let go of our rejection and say, "It's all right, it is only a feeling"—we get a taste of signless liberation. When we see that there is nothing that really lasts, that all is fleeting, flowing, moving, and changing from one moment to the next, we have a moment of freedom. We can practice that with our thoughts, our feelings, or our physical sensations.

As a first step we can become aware of our attachment to the body. Usually, we are concerned whether the body looks good, is dressed appropriately, feels well, eats right, and is comfortable enough. But when we consider the body's fleeting nature, our attachment may wane. We may experience instead a feeling of equanimity. We have no preference whether this body of ours exists or not. This is a moment of real peace, but it doesn't happen by itself. We have to remember again and again that life is not guaranteed but merely supported by *kamma-vipāka* (the results of one's intentions) and that it may run out at any time. That's the reason why the Buddha recommended the daily recollection "I am of the nature to die." We are of this nature all the time, which means right now, not twenty years from now or whenever we feel ready.

Everybody knows they are going to die—there's nothing new about that. The Buddha did not teach anything inaccessible. He asked us to investigate the known in a new way, to get a deep-down feeling that this body cannot remain, no matter how hard we try to keep it. It's a foregone conclusion that we are fighting a losing battle. Of course this doesn't mean we shouldn't look after our bodies. The body has to be washed, fed, and given medicine.

That's all we have to do. And if we can't keep it going indefinitely, that's all right.

One moment of real inner seeing is liberating. The experience of relief and release is totally convincing. It arouses a sense of urgency to practice to the end—to be deterred no longer by the opinions of others or external situations. Liberation is not so difficult that an ordinary person cannot experience it. Were that so, the Buddha's teaching would be in vain.

To get a glimpse of wishless liberation, we can notice the dissatisfaction—the dukkha—that arises in the heart and mind whenever we want something. When we drop the wish, we experience relief. The dukkha does not necessarily arise because we can't fulfill our wish; most likely we can. It's an old axiom that if we want something badly enough, we will get it. The problem is that most people don't know what will bring them happiness. The dukkha, however, lies in the desire itself, which creates tension, a feeling of expectation tinged with worry.

The desire also creates a thought process that is no longer concerned with the here and now, but with the future, with the hope of gratifying the desire. A mind preoccupied with the future cannot attend to the present moment. It lives in the imaginary delusion of what might happen when its desires are fulfilled. Of course, the future hardly ever turns out the way we hope, but, since the real dukkha lies in the wishing itself and not in the outcome, freedom from this kind of wishing is called wishless liberation.

When we deliberately drop our wishes for things, the release and relief generate a feeling of strength. The mind obeys, abandons its old patterns, and a feeling of self-confidence ensues. The more often we drop our wishes, the more powerful the mind becomes. The word "power" has the connotation of power over other people, but here it means power over ourselves. It explains the sort of vibration that emanated from the Buddha and why people flocked to him. We could compare such potential to a powerhouse from which energy can be drawn.

It is useful to aim for a moment of wishless liberation. Our wish could be related to eating, to entertaining ourselves, wanting to go somewhere, buying something, getting information, or talking to someone. Whatever it may be, we can drop it deliberately, knowing that we don't really need it. Letting go of something we want requires willpower. But as soon the mind has dropped its wishes, we can experience the ease of contentment.

To get an inkling of voidness liberation, we can deliberately empty the mind of all it contains, realizing that it has no absolute significance. The less we carry in the mind, the less tired the mind becomes. Usually our minds are full to the brim, which is a great burden for us. Voidness liberation means that there is an absence of all formations (thoughts and reactions). When, for a moment, we have let them go, we can notice how relieved we feel, and we get a taste of voidness liberation. Then we let thoughts and reactions return and realize the difference. Immediately irritation arises, which usually escapes our awareness because we're used to a mind full of formations. We experience the heavy, debilitating, burdensome nature of thoughts only when we are able to compare our usual mind states with momentary emptiness. This may be the first time that we notice the constant sense bombardment we commonly experience.

The most insidious irritations arise through thinking. Thought is a constant process with which we identify and then we act upon. We can't act upon everything we see or hear. If we see a beautiful sunset or hear some great music, there's nothing to do about it, except to like it. No need for a reaction, which may easily result in new problems. Even the most innocuous situations can cause friction if we identify with our thinking process. Once we express our views, hopes, and beliefs, the argument starts, and tears start flowing.

Any meditator knows that the thoughts that arise in the mind have no true significance. When we want to meditate, they are nothing but a nuisance. But the same applies when we don't want to meditate. It makes no difference. Mind is mind.

There is another way of experiencing a moment of voidness. When we see the interconnectedness of dukkha, anicca, and anattā, we glimpse the lack of substance in all existence. We can see the clouds moving in the sky and the wind blowing in the trees. We can notice our blood pulsing and our breath flowing. The universe is contracting and expanding constantly. Within all that movement, we cannot find anything to grasp and retain. There is nothing solid at all anywhere.

Such a moment of seeing frees us from craving and clinging, from samsaric existence with all its dukkha. Clinging is always connected with the fear of losing, and craving is always connected with the fear of not having or not being. Fear and anxiety are natural states of being in the human condition. The supermundane condition is without fear, since there is nothing to be lost or gained.

We crave and cling to whatever we think is important. Being free from craving or clinging for a moment doesn't mean we are indifferent to others. The Buddha's great compassion arose out of his enlightenment. He saw quite clearly that everybody was suffering on account of craving and clinging. Because he had eliminated these mind states within himself, his great compassion was not marred by any concern for himself, and he could completely give himself to others. We can take steps to approach this ideal and get a glimpse of its peacefulness. It is accessible.

Liberation does not happen by grace from above, descending on us like a golden mantle of bliss. It requires moment-to-moment mindfulness and purification until the last speck of impurity has been removed. When we have moments without craving and clinging, we must attend to them with great care and become familiar with them, so that we can repeat them as often as possible. Unless we are fully aware of the contents of our minds, unfortunate moments may predominate. That's why one sees so very few happy people. Happiness is not an accident, it requires hard work.

Just as happiness is an inner condition, so peace is not a sheet of paper that we sign, as if it were a United Nations treaty. If it were, everybody would be peaceful. Peace comes about by letting go. We need to discover where we cling the most and then work with that, whatever it may be. For some of us this is our bodies. We all have to let go of them some day. It would be a good idea to prepare for that day and enjoy the bliss of letting go now, instead of waiting until the last moment.

We prepare ourselves in our practice by realizing moments of liberation. To realize signless liberation, we can fully open up to the experience of a single moment of impermanence, without shying away from it. To realize wishless liberation, we can be aware that every desire creates unsatisfactoriness and irritation, and let go of just one desire. If we could do that at the rate of one per day for the next year, we would change drastically. When we practice letting go of one desire, we can repeat that with the rest of them. Practice makes perfect. The first one is the most difficult.

To realize voidness liberation, we can experience all mental formations as a bombardment of electrical impulses. Some of these impulses come together and make absolutely no sense. If we believe in them and then relate them to others, we start arguing. "How could anybody think like that?" we say to ourselves. We can stop everything for a moment and just be there and experience ease and relief.

Seeing impermanence and unsatisfactoriness in everything brings us to voidness. If there is nothing that remains steady or is satisfactory, then there are only phenomena that have arisen through craving. For instance, this building is here because someone wanted a meditation hall. This person is here because somebody wanted a child. The karma of having been born resulted from wanting to be alive. Everything in existence has arisen because of craving, which is dukkha.

The first instance of penetrating dukkha might create resistance: "What's the use of it all? What am I here for?" Our reason for being is to penetrate the truth of anicca, dukkha, and anattā and avoid repeating the process life after life. Do we really want to go through our whole life experience again, hoping to improve our performance? We will repeat our mistakes until the learning is completed. When we drop whatever is in our minds and experience a moment of freedom, we will know that nothing happens without craving. And we touch emptiness, voidness, and peace through penetration and insight.

We need not worry about what happens after death. We can attend to each moment and learn something new. Everybody has lessons to learn, and if we don't use each day for that, we have lived that day for no purpose. All we have done is kept alive (which is a losing proposition). Our whole life is intended for penetration into wisdom, and each day is our whole life.

24
Path and Fruit

*A*mbition seems to be a natural part of being human. Some people want to be rich, powerful, or famous. Some want to be very knowledgeable and get university degrees. Some want to find a perfect partner, or as nearly perfect as possible. Some just want to find a little niche for themselves, where they can look out the window and see the same scenery every day.

Even when we live in a nunnery, we have ambitions: to become excellent meditators, to be perfectly peaceful, to achieve the rewards of this lifestyle. There is always something to hope for. Instead of being attentive to what is now, we hope for something better to come, maybe tomorrow. Then, when tomorrow arrives, we do the same again. If we were to change this pattern of thinking and attend to what is, we would find something to satisfy us. But if we look for some future thing that is more perfect, more wonderful, more satisfying than what exists right now, we won't find it. We are looking for something that is not there.

The Buddha spoke about two kinds of people, the ordinary worldling *(puthujjana)* and the noble one *(ariya)*. Obviously becoming a noble one is a worthwhile ambition, but if we wait for it to happen at some future time, it will escape us. Only in the recognition of each moment can liberation occur. The difference between a noble one and a worldling is the experience of the "path and fruit" *(magga-phala)* consciousness. The first fruit of this supermundane consciousness is termed stream-entry *(sotāpatti)*, and the person who experiences it is a stream-winner (sotāpanna).

The distinguishing feature of stream-entry is the elimination of the first three fetters binding us to continuous existence. These three are: wrong view of self, skeptical doubt, and belief in rites and rituals. Anyone who is not a stream-winner is chained to these three wrong beliefs and reactions that lead away from freedom into bondage.

Let us take a look at skeptical doubt first. It is that niggling thought in the back of the mind: "There must be an easier way" or "I'm sure I can find happiness somewhere in this wide world." As long as we are doubtful whether the path of liberation leads out of the world and whether satisfaction cannot after all be found within the world, we have no chance of noble attainment, because we are looking in the wrong direction.

Within this world with its people and things, animals and possessions, scenery and sense contacts, there is nothing other than what we already know. If there is more, why is it not easily discernible, why have we not found it? It should be quite plain to see. What are we looking for then?

Obviously we are looking for happiness and peace, just like everyone else. Skeptical doubt, that alarmist, says: "I'm sure if I just handle it a little better than I did last time, I'll be happy. There are a few things I haven't tried yet." Maybe we have not flown our own plane yet or lived in a cave in the Himalayas or sailed around the world or written that best-selling novel. All of these are splendid things to do in the world, but they are a waste of time and energy as far as inner peace is concerned.

Skeptical doubt makes itself felt when we are not quite sure what our next move should be: "Where am I going, what am I to do?" We have not found a direction yet. Skeptical doubt is a fetter that arises in the mind when clarity—the clarity that comes from a path moment—is absent. The consciousness arising from "path and fruit" removes all doubt, because one has experienced the proof oneself. When we bite into the mango, we know its taste. One does not have to force oneself to give up skeptical doubt. What is there to doubt when one has experienced the truth? If one hits oneself with a hammer, one feels pain and cannot doubt it. One knows from one's own experience.

The wrong view of self is the most damaging of the fetters that beset the ordinary person. It contains the deeply imbedded "this is me" notion. There is this "someone" who is meditating. This someone wants to get enlightened, wants to become a stream-winner, wants to be happy. This wrong view of self is the cause of all problems.

As long as somebody is there, that person can have problems. When nobody is there, who could have difficulties? Wrong view of self is the root of all pain, grief, and lamentation. With it also come fears and worries: "Am I going to be all right, happy, and peaceful? Am I going to find what I am looking for, get what I want? Am I going to be healthy, wealthy, and wise?" These worries and fears are well substantiated from our own past. We have not always been healthy, wealthy, and wise, nor got what we wanted, or felt wonderful. So there is very good reason to be worried and fearful as long as the wrong view of self prevails.

Rites and rituals in themselves are not harmful, but believing them to be part of the path to nibbāna is detrimental. They need not even be religious, although we usually think of them in that context—for example, offering flowers and incense at a shrine, prostrating, or celebrating certain festivals and believing that this will accumulate enough merit to go to the deva realms. It is devotion, respect, and gratitude to the Triple Gem (Buddha, Dhamma, Sangha) that count. But rites and rituals are not confined only to religious activities. In our relationships we have certain prescribed ways of acting toward our parents, our children, our partners. How we relate to coworkers, friends, and strangers, how we want to be affirmed by others— all are connected to preconceived ideas of what is right and proper in a certain culture and tradition. None of them contain any basic truth, all are mind-made. The more ideas we have, the less we can see reality. The more we believe in customary, traditional behavior, the harder it is to abandon it when it is not skillful. If we imagine ourselves to be a certain kind of person, we relate to all situations in that way. So ritual is not solely about the way we put flowers on a shrine. It can also dictate how we greet people, if we do so in a certain stereotyped manner rather than simply with an open heart and mind.

These three obstructions fall away when a path and fruit moment has been experienced. There is a marked change in such a person, which is— of course—not externally visible. It would be nice to be able to wear a halo and look blissful, but the change occurs inside. The experience removes all doubt regarding what has to be done in this life. The event is totally differ- ent from anything previously known, so much so that it makes one's life up to that point immaterial. Nothing can be found in the past that has funda- mental importance. The only significant thing to do is go ahead with the practice: to repeat and fortify this experience of the first path moment in oneself. One must relive the initial fruit moment, re-experiencing it over and over until the second path moment can arise. One must repeat what one knows and build on it.

The path and fruit moments recur for the once-returner (sakadāgāmī), the nonreturner (anāgāmī), and the enlightened one (arahant). Each time they make a deeper impact. We could compare this to having examinations at the university. If we go through four years of university study to get a degree, we have to pass examinations at the end of each year. We have to answer questions each time, based on our previously absorbed knowledge. But the questions become more intricate and more difficult with each subsequent examination. While they are always concerned with the same subject, they require more depth of understanding each time, until we finally graduate and do not have to return to university. It is the same with our spiritual development. Each path moment is based on the previous one and is concerned with the same subject, yet it goes deeper and further, until we pass our final test and need not return.

The path moment does not have any thinking or feeling in it. It is not comparable to the meditative absorptions (jhāna), although it is based on them (only the concentrated mind can enter into a path moment). It does not have the same qualities. The meditative absorptions have—in their initial stages—the ingredients of rapture, happiness, and peacefulness. Later on, the mind experiences expansion, nothingness, and a change of perception. The path moment does not contain any of these states of mind. It has a quality of nonbeing. This comes as such a relief and changes one's world view so totally that it is quite understandable that the Buddha insisted on the distinction between a worldling and a noble one. While the meditative absorptions bring feelings of oneness and unity, the path moment leaves such feelings behind. The subsequent moment of fruition understands experience with a totally new vision.

The new understanding recognizes every thought and every feeling as stress (dukkha). The most elevated thought, the most sublime feeling still has this quality. Only when there is nothing is there no stress. Nothing— no internal or external thing—has the quality of total satisfactoriness. Once one sees this, one's passion for wanting anything dies away. One sees all things for what they really are, and one knows that nothing can give the happiness that arises through the practice of the path.

This nibbānic element cannot be truly described as bliss, because the word "bliss" connotes exhilaration. We use this word for the meditative absorptions, where it refers to a sense of excitement. The nibbānic element does not recognize bliss because all that arises is seen as stress. The phrase "the bliss of nibbāna" may give one the impression that one may find perfect happiness, but the opposite is true. One finds that there is nothing—no more unhappiness, only peace.

To look for the path and fruit moments will not bring them about, because only moment-to-moment awareness can do so. This awareness will eventually culminate in real concentration, where one can let go of thinking and be totally absorbed. We can drop the meditation subject at that time. We need not push it aside, it falls away of its own accord, and absorption in awareness occurs. If there has to be an ambition in one's life, this is the only worthwhile one. No others will bring fulfillment.

Rites and rituals cease for a stream-enterer because the person who has experienced a path moment under no circumstances indulges in any role-playing. All roles are the ingredients of unreality. One may continue to observe religious rites because they contain aspects of respect, gratitude, and devotion. But one no longer relates to people or situations through rituals or stories that one has invented. Instead one will act out of a spontaneous, open heart.

Letting go of the wrong view of self is—of course—the most profound change. For the stream-winner the wrong view of self can never arise again, but feelings associated with it can because the path moment has been singular and fleeting. It has not made a complete impact yet. Had it done so, it would have resulted in enlightenment. It is possible (the Buddha's discourses mention this) for all four stages of holiness to be realized while listening to one exposition of the Dhamma.

It is useful to remind ourselves in all waking moments that body, feeling, perception, mental formations, and consciousness have no core substance, are all impermanent, changing from moment to moment. Whether we have had a direct vision of nonself or just an understanding of it, we have to bring that realization back into our minds and relive it as often as possible. As we continue to do this, ordinary problems become less of an obstruction. If we remain aware of the impermanence of all that exists, our difficulties seem far less important, and the view of self subtly changes.

The view we have of ourselves is our worst enemy. Everyone has invented a persona, a mask that one wears, and we do not want to see what is behind it. We do not allow anyone else to look either. After having had a path moment, we no longer feel the need to maintain our persona. But without that experience if anyone should even try to look behind our mask, fear and rejection come to the fore. The best antidote is to remember again and again that there is really nobody there, only phenomena. Even though our inner vision may not be developed enough to substantiate such a claim, the affirmation helps us to loosen our grasp and cling a little less tightly.

The direction of the practice is certainly toward stream-entry. However, there is nothing to get, and everything to give up. Unless we relinquish all we cling to, the moment cannot happen, and we will continue to live the same way we always have—beset and obstructed by dukkha, and subject to praise and blame, loss and gain, fame and disrepute, happiness and unhappiness. The usual problems—all caused by "self"—will arise again and again. The real change begins with a decisive alteration in the way we view ourselves. Otherwise the difficulties remain, recreated by the same unchanged person.

We can read about disenchantment and dispassion as steps on the path to liberation and freedom. They cannot have meaning and impact unless we have a vision of a totally different reality, one that does not contain the world's manifoldness. When we sit in meditation and start thinking, this is mental diversification and expansion (papañca). The nibbānic element is unitary, not manifold. One could say that it is empty of all that we know. Until we see it, the world will keep calling. But we need not believe it all. This is a difficult task, and we must remind ourselves of this often, lest we get caught in temptation.

Certainly we can experience pleasure from the senses. If we have good karma, there will be many occasions—delicious food, beautiful scenery, pleasant people, good music, interesting books, a comfortable home, not too much physical discomfort. But do these bring utter fulfillment? Since they have not done so in the past, why should they in the future? Path and fruit bring fulfillment because they are empty of phenomena. Emptiness neither changes nor becomes unpleasant, and it cannot lack peace since there is nothing to disturb it.

When people hear or read about nibbāna, they are apt to say, "How can I want nothing?" When one has seen, however, that every single want we have is meant to fill an inner void and dissatisfaction, then the time has come to want nothing. Wanting nothing goes beyond not wanting, because one now accepts the reality that there is nothing worthwhile to be had. Wanting nothing makes it possible to experience that actually there *is* nothing—only peace.

Being mindfully aware in and out of meditation is the practice that brings results. It means doing one thing at a time, attentive to mind and body. When listening to Dhamma, just listen. When sitting in meditation, just attend to the meditation subject. When planting a tree, just plant. No frills, no judgments. This habituates the mind to be in each moment. Only in such a way can a path moment occur, here and now. There is no reason why an intelligent, healthy, committed person should not be able to attain it with patience and perseverance.

Glossary

The following Pali words encompass concepts for which there are no adequate synonyms in English. The explanations of these terms have been adapted from the *Buddhist Dictionary* by Nyanatiloka Mahathera (Kandy: Buddhist Publication Society, 1980).

anāgāmī. Non-Returner, a noble disciple in the third stage of holiness

anagarika. Person temporarily observing the eight precepts

anattā. Nonself, non-ego, egolessness, impersonality. "Neither within the bodily and mental phenomena of existence, nor outside of them can be found anything that in the ultimate sense could be regarded as a self-existing, real ego-identity, soul, or any other abiding substance."

anicca. Impermanence, a basic feature of all conditioned phenomena, be they material or mental, coarse or subtle, one's own or external

anusaya. The seven proclivities, inclinations, or tendencies

arahant. A holy one. Through the extinction of all defilements, he reaches already in this very life the deliverance of mind, the deliverance through wisdom, which he himself has understood and realized.

ariya. Noble ones, noble persons

avijjā. Ignorance, nescience, unknowing, synonymous with delusion; the primary root of all evil and suffering in the world, veiling our mental eyes and preventing us from seeing the true nature of things

bhavarāga. Craving for continued existence; one of the seven tendencies

brahma-vihāra. The four sublime abodes: loving-kindness, compassion, altruistic joy, and equanimity

citta. Mind, heart, consciousness

citta-viveka. Mental detachment, inner detachment from sensuous things

deva. Heavenly being, deity, celestial being who lives in a happy world but is not freed from the cycle of existence

Dhamma. The liberating law discovered and proclaimed by the Buddha, summed up in the Four Noble Truths; dhamma (lower case): phenomenon, object of mind

diṭṭhi. View, belief, speculative opinion; except in the case of "right view," refers to wrong and negative view or opinion

dukkha. In common usage, pain, painful feeling, which may be physical or mental; in Buddhist usage, suffering, ill, the unsatisfactory nature and general insecurity of all conditioned phenomena

jhāna. Meditative absorptions, tranquility meditation

kalyāṇamitta. Noble or good friend; a senior monk who is the mentor and friend of his pupil wishing for his welfare and concerned with his progress, guiding his meditation; in particular the meditation teacher

kamma/karma. Action. Denotes the wholesome and unwholesome volitions and their concomitant mental factors, causing rebirth and shaping the character of beings and thereby their destiny. The term does not signify the result of actions and most certainly not the deterministic fate of man.

kammaṭṭhāna. Lit. "working-ground" (i.e., for meditation); the term in the commentaries for subjects of meditation

kāya-viveka. Bodily detachment; abiding in solitude free from alluring sensuous objects

khandha. The five groups of physical and mental phenomena, which appear to the ordinary person as the basis of his/her ego or personality: body, feeling, perception, mental formations, and consciousness

lokiya. Mundane; all those states of consciousness and mental factors arising in the worldling, as well as in the noble one, which are not associated with the supermundane

lokuttara. Supermundane, a term for the four paths and four fruitions

magga-phala. Path and fruit. The path-consciousness arises first, immediately followed by "fruition," a moment of supermundane awareness.

māna. Conceit, pride; one of the ten fetters binding to existence, also one of the underlying tendencies

Māra. The Buddhist "tempter" figure; the personification of negativity and passions, of the totality of worldly existence and of death

mettā. Loving-kindness, one of the four sublime emotions (brahma-vihāra)

nibbāna. Lit. extinction, to cease blowing, to become extinguished. Nibbāna constitutes the highest and ultimate goal of all Buddhist aspirations. It is the absolute extinction of that life-grasping will manifested as greed, hate, and delusion, and thereby the absolute deliverance from all future rebirth.

nīvaraṇa. Hindrances, five mental obstacles that blind our mental vision and obstruct concentration: sensual desire, ill will, sloth and torpor, restlessness and worry, and skeptical doubt

paññā. Wisdom

papañca. Proliferation, lit. "expansion, diffuseness"; detailed exposition, development, manifoldness, multiplicity, differentiation

paṭiccasamuppāda. Dependent origination, the doctrine of the conditionality of all physical and psychical phenomena

puthujjana. Lit. "one of the many folk" worldling, ordinary man, anyone still possessed of all the ten fetters binding to the round of rebirths

sacca. Truth; one of the Four Noble Truths

sakadāgāmī. Once-returner; one who has shed the five lower fetters and who reappears in a higher world to reach nibbāna *sakkāya-diṭṭhi.* Personality-belief, the first of the ten fetters, abandoned at stream-entry

samatha. Tranquility, serenity; synonym of *samādhi* (concentration)

saṃsāra. Round of rebirth, lit. "perpetual wandering"; designates the restless sea of life

sammā-diṭṭhi. Right understanding.

saṃvega. a sense of urgency

Sangha. Lit. congregation, the name for the community of monks and nuns. As the third of the Three Gems and the Three Refuges, it applies to the community of the noble ones (ariya).

sankhāra. formation, mental formations and kamma formations; sometimes refers to bodily functions or mental functions; also may refer to anything formed

sati. Mindfulness, the seventh step on the Noble Eightfold Path; the first of the seven factors of enlightenment

sīla. Morality

sīlabbata-parāmāsa. Attachment to mere rules and rituals, the third fetter and one of the four kinds of clinging, which disappears on attaining to stream-entry

sotāpanna. Stream-enterer, the first attainment of a noble disciple

sotāpatti. Stream-entry, the first attainment of becoming a noble one.

sukha. Meditative happiness, a feature of the first and second meditative absorptions

sutta. Discourse by the Buddha or one of his enlightened disciples

Tiratana. Three Jewels; the Buddha, Dhamma, and Sangha

vicikicchā. Skeptical doubt, one of the five mental hindrances and one of the three fetters, which disappears forever at stream-entry

vipāka. Karmic results

vipassanā. Insight into the truth of the impermanence, suffering, and impersonality of all corporeal and mental phenomena

yathā-bhūta-ñāṇadassana. Knowledge and vision according to reality, one of the eighteen chief kinds of insight

About the Author

Ayya Khema was born in Berlin in 1923 to Jewish parents. In 1938 she escaped from Germany and was taken to Glasgow, Scotland. Her parents went to China, where Ayya Khema later joined them. With the outbreak of war they were put into a Japanese concentration camp, where her father died.

Ayya Khema later emigrated to the United States. Between 1960 and 1964 she traveled with her husband and son throughout Asia, where she learned meditation. Ten years later she began to teach meditation in Europe, America, and Australia. She was ordained as a Buddhist nun in Sri Lanka in 1979 by Narada Maha Thera.

In 1978 she established a Theravada forest monastery, near Sydney, Australia with Phra Khantipalo. In Sri Lanka she set up the International Buddhist Women's Centre in Colombo and Parappuduwa Nun's Island.

In 1987 Ayya Khema coordinated the first ever international conference of Buddhist nuns, where H.H. the Dalai Lama was the keynote speaker. In May 1987 she was the first person ever to address the United Nations in New York on the topic of Buddhism.

She served as the spiritual director of Buddha-Haus in Germany, which she established in 1989, until her death, and in June 1997 she founded the first Theravada monastery in Germany.

Ayya Khema wrote over twenty-five books on meditation and the Buddha's teaching; her work has been translated into more than seven languages. Her *Being Nobody, Going Nowhere* received the Christmas Humphreys Award.

Venerable Ayya Khema died in Germany on November 2, 1997.

Also from Wisdom

Henepola Gunaratana

MINDFULNESS IN PLAIN ENGLISH

This step-by-step guide to Insight meditation is truly practical and direct. Venerable Gunaratana's conversational style and use of everyday examples imbue the basic teachings of Vipassana meditation with unsurpassable clarity and wit.

"This work will be of great value...especially to people without access to a teacher."—Larry Rosenberg, author of *Breath by Breath: The Liberating Practice of Insight Meditation*

208 pages, isbn 0-86171-064-9, $14.95

THE LONG DISCOURSES OF THE BUDDHA
A Translation of the Digha Nikaya
Translated by Maurice Walshe

An invaluable collection of the teachings of the Buddha that reveal his gentleness, compassion, and penetrating wisdom. These thirty-four discourses are among the oldest records of the Buddha's original teachings. (Previously titled *Thus Have I Heard)*

656 pages, isbn 0-86171-103-3, $37.50

THE MIDDLE LENGTH DISCOURSES OF THE BUDDHA
A New Translation of the Majjhima Nikaya
Translated by Bhikkhu Ñanamoli & Bhikkhu Bodhi

1995 Outstanding Academic Book Award—*Choice Magazine*

Tricycle Prize for Excellence in Buddhist Publishing for "Dharma Discourse"

The 152 discourses of this major collection combine a rich variety of contextual settings with deep and comprehensive teachings.

"...remarkable both in its scope and in its contemporary rendering of the Buddha's words."—*Tricycle: The Buddhist Review*

1424 pages, isbn 0-86171-072-x, $60.00

Nyanaponika Thera and Hellmuth Hecker

GREAT DISCIPLES OF THE BUDDHA
Their Lives, Their Works, Their Legacy
Edited with an introduction by Bhikkhu Bodhi

Great Disciples of the Buddha is a compilation of twenty-four life stories of the closest and most eminent of the Buddha's personal disciples. The profiles, set against the colorful social and cultural background of ancient India, bring to life such near-legendary names as Sāriputta and Moggallāna, Ānanda and Mahākassapa.

"I am grateful for the publication of this book...I recommend *Great Disciples* to friends and students alike."—Thich Nhat Hanh, author of *Living Buddha, Living Christ*

"A truly excellent and unique new addition to the literature from the Pali texts."—Jack Kornfield, author of *A Path with Heart*

448 pages, isbn 0-86171-128-9, $29.95

Also by Ayya Khema

WHO IS MY SELF?
A Guide to Buddhist Meditation

In this beautifully crafted guide through a discourse of the Buddha, the Venerable Ayya Khema will lead you, as the Buddha led his disciple Poṭṭhapāda, through progressively higher levels of understanding and realization of the true nature of the "self" and consciousness. Interpreting this famous discourse of the Buddha with clear and insightful examples from her years of teaching meditation, she will guide you along the path of perhaps the most effective Buddhist meditative practice for personal transformation.

"*Who Is My Self* is a truly astonishing book. It discusses, for the first time as far as I know, in definite and practical language, the well-known eight stages of absorption, based not on textual sources but on personal experience. If you are interested in Buddhist meditation in all its color, depth, and refinement you will want to pay close attention to this book."
—Zoketsu Norman Fischer, Co-Abbot, San Francisco Zen Center

192 pages, isbn 0-86171-127-0, $14.95

BEING NOBODY, GOING NOWHERE
Meditations on the Buddhist Path

"This book is a valuable guide along the path of meditative insight and loving compassion. It is direct, clear, and inspiring."—Sharon Salzberg

"Not just highly recommended but essential reading for hearts inclined to the path."—Dharmacrafts

192 pages, isbn 0-86171-052-5, $14.95

About Wisdom

Wisdom Publications, a not-for-profit publisher, is dedicated to making available authentic Buddhist works for the benefit of all. We publish translations of the sutras and tantras, commentaries and teachings of past and contemporary Buddhist masters, and original works by the world's leading Buddhist scholars. We publish our titles with the appreciation of Buddhism as a living philosophy and with the special commitment to preserve and transmit important works from all the major Buddhist traditions.

If you would like more information or a copy of our mail-order catalog, please contact us at:

Wisdom Publications
199 Elm Street
Somerville, Massachusetts 02144 USA
Telephone: (617) 776-7416
Fax: (617) 776-7841
Email: info@wisdompubs.org
Web Site: http://www.wisdompubs.org

The Wisdom Trust

As a not-for-profit publisher, Wisdom Publications is dedicated to the publication of fine Dharma books for the benefit of all sentient beings and dependent upon the kindness and generosity of sponsors in order to do so. If you would like to make a donation to Wisdom Publications, please do so through our Somerville office. If you would like to sponsor the publication of a book, please write or email us for more information.

Thank you.

Wisdom Publications is a non-profit, charitable 501(c)(3) organization and a part of the Foundation for the Preservation of the Mahayana Tradition (FPMT).